To Long Shadow,
for all your Loved Ones
you have lost.

Golden Spirit
x

July 2018

Lessons from Loved Ones in Heaven

How to Connect with your Loved One on the Other Side to Heal from Loss

Brent Atwater

Just Plain Love® Books
inspiring thoughts that provide smiles, hugs and healing for every reader's heart!

Brent Atwater's *Just Plain Love*® Book is given

To: _____

Message: _____
_____

with
LOTS of LOVE
and
HUGS!!!

From: _____

Date:_____

Copyright information © 2000-2018 by B. Brent Atwater

Published and Distributed in the United States by:

Just Plain Love® Books, Brent Atwater
www.BrentAtwater.com
Editorial: Brent Atwater   Cover Design: Brent Atwater
Interior Design: Brent Atwater   Illustrations: Brent Atwater

All rights reserved. No part of this book may be reproduced by any mechanical, photographic or electronic process or in the form of a phonographic reading: nor may it be stored in a retrieval system transmitted, or otherwise be copied for public or private use- other than for "fair use" as brief quotations embodied in articles and reviews without prior written permission of the publisher and author.
  The author of this book, Brent Atwater, is not a medical doctor nor associated with any branch of allopathic medicine. ALWAYS consult a physician or trained health care professional either directly or indirectly concerning any physical or medical problem or condition before undertaking any diet, health related technique or lifestyle change program.
  The contents presented herein are derived from the author's intuition and experiences. The intent of the author is only to offer information of a general nature to help facilitate your journey to health and well-being. In the event you choose to use any of the information in this book for yourself, which is your constitutional right, as in traditional medicine, there are no guarantees and the author and the publisher assume no responsibility for your actions.

Library of Congress Cataloging-in-Publication Data
ISBN-13:978-1974035335
ISBN-10: 1974035336
Hardcover ISBN:
Kindle ASIN:
eBook ISBN
Audio Book:

This book is translated into other languages and available in print and eBooks at most online retailers.

R 2018

Dedication

This book is written to honor my entire inspiring and
beloved canine, feline, equine and other animal teachers,
guardians and companions
(including "Fishy") with whom
I shared my experiences, learning and life.
From my heart and soul to yours, thank you!

My special love goes to each of you
for filling my life and heart with joy.

To Thomas Michael Ramseur Wellford,
whose life, love and passing made my understanding
possible.
I shall always hold you and hear you in my heart,
my soul and my dreams. To those very special people and
fur babies who are my joy, and with whom I share hope,
laughter and LIFE!!!

Acknowledgements

I want to thank you for taking the time to explore my Just Plain Love® Books and for allowing me to share what I have learned and am learning about loss, death, life after death, communication and connection with the Other Side through my personal experiences and those of other individuals.

Special thanks to Michael Wellford and my precious fur, finned and feathered companions for their contributions and enduring patience with me and my spiritual path.

It is my intent that this information will facilitate inspiration, provide comfort, support, greater perspectives and answer your questions through expanded awareness.

I thank those who have supported and encouraged my journey and the authors, speakers and teachers who contributed to shaping my consciousness.

A special thank you to all Spirits on the Other Side who's NEVER ending love bond represents why I write my books.

Special Gratitude

To Frankie Johnson and Mona Samet for their support, suggestions and contributions to my book. Many thanks for fabulous photographs and support by Dianne Virga.
To David Mathews, thank you for real cheese choice discussions.

To all the administrators of my Facebook groups who volunteer to reach out, inspire, support, uplift and expand awareness to help heal hearts every day, I want to thank each of you for all you do for others. Namaste.

Special hugs to Christie, Mike and Kennedy Hepfner for their guidance, insights and help with practical and real day to day questions and input about dealing and coping with a loss. More thanks to Kennedy for her steady hand, artistic eagle eye, fashion savvy and patience while producing my videos, plus providing fabulous ideas, and keeping me "with it."

To all my "voices," Guides and other energies and entities who serve the Christ White Light named and unnamed who are relentless, impatient, persistent, exhausting, exasperating, informative, accurate, edgy, humorous, entertaining, deliberate, persuasive, detailed beyond belief and always of the highest integrity and utmost determination to help me and my clients for our highest and best good.

I admire their patience with my path, their directives for my education and evolution and their ongoing and forever training of my soul.

They are my best friends, greatest teachers, constant companions, best protectors, collaborators and support team.
Namaste! all y'all.

Lessons from Loved Ones in Heaven
How to Connect with your Loved One on the Other Side
to Heal from Loss

Table of Contents

Gift Message	5
Dedication	7
Acknowledgements	9
Special Gratitude	10
Table of Contents	13

Introduction- Honoring Your Loved One	17

Chapter 1- Get Your Mind Right

What do I do Now???	19
Stages of Grief Chart	23
Coping with the Loss of a Loved One	25
Determine Where You are Right Now	27
Examine the Time You have on Earth	33
Recovery Starts in Your Mind	33
How to Make Choices to Change Your Life	37
Choose How You Respond	39
Choose to ACT	42
Act Right Now	43
Change Negative into Positive	44
Self-Monitoring	47
"It's My Choice"	49

Chapter 2- Understanding Physical Death

Transition	53
What is a Memory Moment?	55
Death is Transition to a New Life	59
The Progression of Transition	63

Chapter 3- Beginning a New Journey
Spirits	69
Why Connect with Spirit?	75
Information about Connecting	77
How to Connect with Spirit	79
What Interferes with Connection	82
Most Important	83
How to Pray	85
Protection Prayer	87

Chapter 4- How to Connect with Your Loved One
Types of Spirit Connections	89
Signs from the Afterlife & Other Side	91
How Spirits decide What Signs to Send	93
Excessive Grief Affects Signs	96
How to Ask for Signs	99
How to Touch & Feel Spirit Energy	101
Sharing Space with Spirits	107
Being with Spirit on Demand	111

Dreams	171
How to Ask Spirit to Visit in Dreams	121
How to Ask a Specific Question in a Dream	122

Stronger Spirit Connections	125
Types of Visitation	127
Seeing Spirits	131
How to See a Spirit	133
Prayer to See Spirit	134
Request for More Information	137

Communication with Spirit	139
Start the Conversation	143
How to Talk with a Specific Spirit	145
Communication Prayer	151

How to Close a Session	154
Communication Mistakes	156

Chapter 5- Rebuilding Your Life

Identify Your Feelings	159
Shock & Numbness	159
Hurt	161
Anniversaries and Special Occasions	163
Loneliness	167
Isolation	169
Express Your Feelings	171
Support Groups	173
"Whatever- land"	179
Stress and Anxiety	189
Anger	193
Depression	197
Memorial Area:	201
Memorials	201
Tattoos	205
Creating an Uplifting Environment	207
Guilt	217
Dealing with Loss by Suicide.	220
Suicidal Thoughts	221
Emptiness	225
New Relationships	227

Refining Your Rebuilding	229
State of Mind Determines Quality of Life	231
In Conclusion	233

Book Clubs	234
Message to Individuals	234
Resources for Healing Your Heart	235
Brent Atwater	239
Friend	243
Just Plain Love® Books	247

Lessons from Loved Ones in Heaven
How to Connect with your Loved One on the Other Side
to Heal from Loss

Introduction
Honoring Your Loved One

The funeral is over, you've left the vet's office or you've picked up the ashes. You ask yourself, did I honor their wishes?

Whether a Person or Pet, it's important to know that you did the absolute best you could with the circumstances and time that you had, even if it was a sudden or horrific event like Mike's car crash.

Mike wanted to be cremated and spread over the ocean where he sailed. Because I was **only** the fiancé and not a real family member, his family decided to bury his ashes in a family plot without any marking. I became **obsessed** with honoring Mike's wishes and incensed there was no marble headstone.

I plotted how to drive 4 hours to his gravesite, pretend I was planting a bush, while snatching his remains and running off to spread them as he wanted. Needless to say, excavating interred remains from a cemetery plot that is not yours is against the law.
That wasn't going to stop me!

On my first attempt, everything was packed, bushes and all and ready to go. Out of the blue, I had a flat rear tire while my car was sitting in the garage. After I got it fixed, there wasn't enough time to make the daylight run and get back as if I had gone nowhere!

Six months later, I coerced a friend to go with me. We got 2.5 hours out of town and the engine on my impeccably maintained car started spewing smoke. After waiting for what seemed like hours for AAA, we limped home foiled again!

My third try was 2 years later so no one would remember what I was really up to.
Bushes, shovel, travel snacks, gas full, car and tires prechecked all ready to go. I'm smiling like a Cheshire cat. I turn the ignition and my car wouldn't start. DAMN! It was like the Universe was against me doing anything.

Mike quietly said, "It doesn't matter, I'm not dead nor in that Urn."

I had a lot to learn. It was time for me to release my preconceived concept of death.

In order to continue our never-ending love, I needed to discover, understand and experience connecting and communicating with Mike in a different way to validate and resume our life together!

Chapter 1- Get Your Mind Right

What do I do Now???

You probably need a GREAT BIG HUG!!! and some guidance.

I get it! You are in a raw, gut wrenching place while probably feeling numb, devastated and don't know what to do or where to turn after your loss. You're not going crazy and you're NOT alone anymore! I **totally** understand your position, **we'll get through this together.**

I fought my way through the transition experience, made it back into life and so can you!

My fiancé Mike was killed in a head on car collision just 3 hours after he said, "I'll see you around 9:30 pm." My world and dreams were shattered, my heart ripped from my chest, my soul blown to oblivion and my mind, who knows where that went.

I have lost numerous soul Pets too, all creating the same response because they are "family" and truth be told, sometimes closer than some family!

I have lived the experience you are going through.

Lessons from Loved Ones in Heaven
How to Connect with your Loved One on the Other Side
to Heal from Loss

Death and loss changed the course of my life and my life's purpose. I promised God to honor Mike's transition by dedicating my life to helping others so they would not be alone during this horrific time.

The pain of death whether a person or a pet etches your soul and changes your being.
For over 20 years I have assisted individuals and pet parents on their healing journey from grief through recovery and then rebuilding their reentry into life.

I have lived the struggles. I had to pull myself up by my bootstraps to survive the emotional hell you're faced with after Death. It's not an easy journey and some of the mental speed bumps will be hard to implement. I promise the end result will be worth your efforts. Your life will have purpose and meaning again.

On the upcoming pages, I offer step by step practical, powerful, profound advice and guided healing solutions from my heart and soul's "experiences" during sickness, degenerating health, disease, chronic illness and even sudden or inevitable death. And, from all the research I did to get me through dealing with Mike's death.

I've comforted, supported and helped people and pets who were dying and assisted their transition. Then I talked with, listened to and shared their communication, messages and directives from Heaven and the Other Side.

Many thanks to all those beloved Beings who have taught me from the Afterlife what I share in this book. You **can** move forward after suffering the loss of a beloved person or pet and They want you to do so.

Ignore people that think you are "crazy" because **you feel** that there is more to life than the finality of Death, i.e. dead and done. **You're in charge of doing what it takes to survive and evolve.**

From this moment on, your goal is to make choices that create comfort, clarity, understanding, healing, happiness, peace, closure and a fulfilling quality of life.
This book will help renovate your heart throughout your recovery!

A reader remarked "Brent Atwater's books make you think a LOT!" I hope this one does too so you have a new understanding and awareness of "all there is!"

I'm not writing this book to be a "warm and fuzzy" read. I'm tackling the hard and harsh reality to guide you out of that emptiness. There could be lessons you'll find difficult to embrace in order to change. Change is always a challenge. It won't be easy since life as you knew it has been overturned.

Before I make a video, do a live event or write a book, I always ask God to help me reach, teach and touch the hearts of those I came to serve. There are no guarantees with any of the suggested solutions. Use only the recommendations that resonate with you.

This following chart will help you identify your current stage of Grief. At the end of this book we'll check again.

Lessons from Loved Ones in Heaven
How to Connect with your Loved One on the Other Side
to Heal from Loss

STAGES OF GRIEF

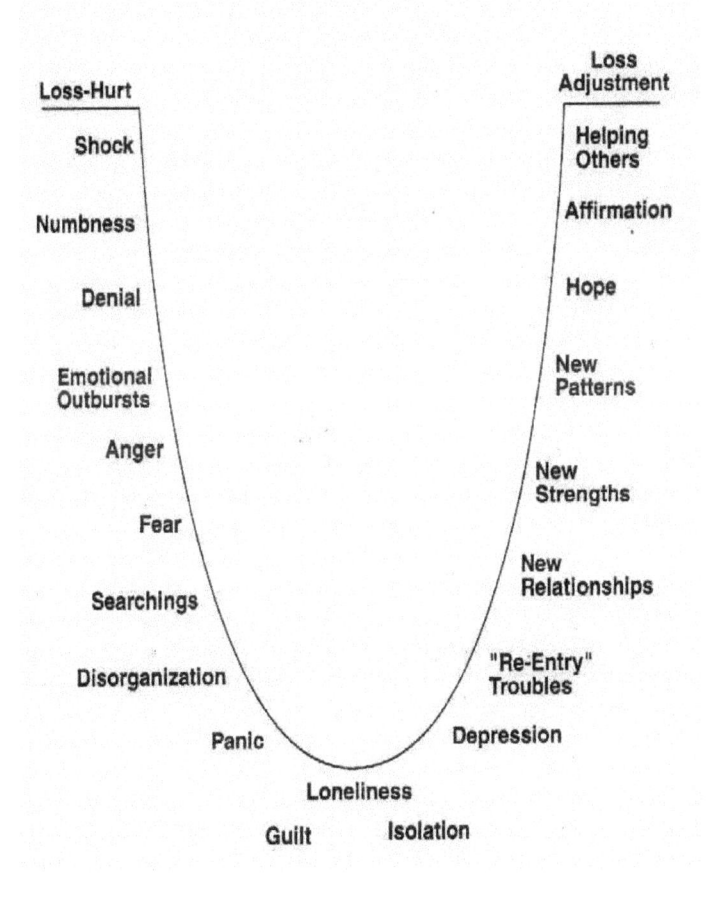

Loss-Hurt
- Shock
- Numbness
- Denial
- Emotional Outbursts
- Anger
- Fear
- Searchings
- Disorganization
- Panic

Loss Adjustment
- Helping Others
- Affirmation
- Hope
- New Patterns
- New Strengths
- New Relationships
- "Re-Entry" Troubles
- Depression

Loneliness

Guilt   Isolation

Lessons from Loved Ones in Heaven
How to Connect with your Loved One on the Other Side
to Heal from Loss

Coping with the Loss of a Loved One

The American Cancer Society's article states, "Grief is complicated. If normal mourning does not occur, or if the mourning goes on for a long time without any progress, it's called "complicated grief" or "unresolved grief." Symptoms might include:

* Continued disbelief in the death of the loved one, or emotional numbness over the loss.

* Unable to accept the death.

* Feeling preoccupied with the loved one or how they died.

* Intense sorrow and emotional pain, sometimes including bitterness or anger.

* Unable to enjoy good memories about the loved one.

* Blaming oneself for the death.

* Wishing to die to be with the loved one.

* Excessively avoiding reminders of their loss.

* Continuous yearning and longing for the deceased.

Feeling alone, detached from others, or distrustful of others since the death.

* Trouble pursuing interests or planning for the future after the death of the loved one.

* Feeling that life is meaningless or empty without the loved one.

* Loss of identity or purpose in life, feeling like part of themselves died with the loved one.

For some people who are taking care of a person or pet with a long-term illness, complicated grief can actually start while their loved one is still alive. Caregivers under severe stress, especially if the outlook is bleak, may be at higher risk of having abnormal grief even before the death.

If you or anyone close to the deceased has any of the above symptoms of major depression or complicated grief, talk with a qualified health or mental health professional. Treatments have been shown to help people with complicated grief. Treatment is important, since people with complicated grief are at risk of getting worse.

Determine Where You are Right Now!

Your healing starts now. You need to be real and authentic with yourself to get **you** back! Read the symptoms on the previous pages and be real if any apply. This process builds on each block of reality that you change, replace or honor in your life.
You're renovating piece by piece. That's why we're not tackling everything all at once. Let's start at the bottom of the hole in your soul and remodel our way out!

I kept notes during my journey to stay in tune with my feelings and to document my progress. WHY? Because this can be a roller coaster ride with feelings and reactions all over the place. Our goal, regenerate a new you, in your new world.

First, identify where you are emotionally at this very moment. Then you will have a real starting point. Let yourself feel the pain and all the other emotions, too. Don't tell yourself how to feel in the beginning or let others tell you how you should feel. This is your journey and start only when you are ready to begin.

Be patient with the process. Don't pressure yourself with expectations. Accept that you need to experience your pain, your emotions, and your own way of healing – all in your own time. Don't judge your emotions or compare yourself to others.

Remember that no one else can tell you how you should mourn or when to stop until you are ready for help.

It took me over 7 years to get real with myself and move forward. Deep down I believed that I was NOT honoring Mike's life if I gave up grieving, set aside his things -like take off my engagement ring which I clung to ferociously, tried to suppress his memory and moved on with my life. With pets, I slept holding their collars and cuddling in their blankets and swore to never love another.

At that time, I didn't know any better.
I didn't realize I could still cherish him in my heart, honor our life, connect and communicate daily and still have a new fulfilling life of my own.

The pain of death is a very special type of pain in your life and being. That's why whether a person or pet, it's victims experience the same devastating horrific soul shattering loss. Acknowledge your feelings, even the ones you don't like. Let yourself cry. You need to do both for healing.

I cried, yelled at, argued and bargained with and was angry about Mike's passing. I made any offering and every deal I could to the Universe to right his death.

Months of dropping out of life and living in "Whatever" land didn't work.
Excess wine and food didn't work.
Isolating myself and staring into space from under the covers didn't work.
Crying, screaming and having tantrums didn't work.
I even told the Universe it could take me, because I didn't want to stay on Earth without him. The Universe told me I had a job to do, so I had to stay.

There was **nothing** else to do or turn to in order to right this situation. No amount of reexamining every little detail to see if I missed something that could have changed the outcome or brought him back. Physical Death has no do overs. And when an assistant minister said, "look for the gift in Mike's death," I told him to go to a place that wasn't Heaven and walked out slamming the office door in his face. I was angry! How disrespectful of him!

MANY YEARS LATER (I'm a slow learner) it dawned on me, it was up to me, to change the misery, suffering and vacuous life that was happening **to me**. (that's a major key - being a victim of what was happening to me by my own choice.)

I had to meet me where I was and get real about choosing to move forward.

The second step is to determine if you really want to recover from your grief and what's "happening to you." Just because you decide to move forward doesn't mean you want to give up your grief and suffering lifestyle.

Some folks don't think they can live without grief and others can't fathom how healing is possible. Some even choose the victim mode for attention and identity.
Be honest with yourself.

I ask again, do you **really** want to stop grieving and live again? It'll take determination, stamina and sensitivity.
You CAN do this!

Having a new awareness and understanding that loss and death is just transition out of the earth suit/ body into a different energy form, will change your grief.

I know that changing thought patterns will probably shake up your foundation and make you question core beliefs that you were taught.

Now is the time for YOU to examine the views you inherited.
Then create, evolve and develop core beliefs that

resonate with your new awareness, emotions and lifestyle.

How do you accomplish that? Sometimes that's where people balk and stop. They do not want to change what they have been preconditioned to think, taught by their family or peers or reschooled outside of or in addition to their religious beliefs. They don't want to step out of or expand their current belief foundation comfort zone.

This is where they quit. Some individuals believe it's easier to hold onto the concept that a person is dead and that their pet is waiting for them in Heaven or Rainbow Bridge. It's their choice (key word) of denial and shutting down having to deal with death even if there may be viable and happier alternatives to consider.
Sticking your head in the sand at this point does not serve your heart well.

For people that embrace the dead and gone belief, I honor your choice. (key word). However, that dead end concept causes a lot of unnecessary suffering, lack of clarity and closure plus ongoing subliminal grief residue for the **rest** of their life.

We'll go on a healing and learning journey that upgrades your mind so you can understand why the death occurred and be able to enjoy communicating and connecting with people and pets from Heaven, the Other Side, Afterlife, the Universe, etc. while you're still alive and well on Earth.

Your new reality and understanding of physics will give you a positive perspective about the Transition (key word) process.

You need to be fully invested in your healing and recovery to be successful. If you encounter a backslide, its ok and normal. I'm the best example of a person who did NOT get it for years UNTIL I got it! The only time frame we're looking at for recovery is the one that you are comfortable with. Just go back and redo the steps again and again until you're ready to add the next layer to expand yourself.

If you think I'm being pushy, I am!
I'm trying to nudge you forward more rapidly that I evolved. I don't want you to suffer the unnecessary pain I endlessly endured because I didn't know any better.

I've learned to know that Mike's Spirit is near almost every day and I know he wants me to be happy. He provides ongoing input on my important decisions and continuously offers perspectives and directives to make my life better. His help is **always** there whenever I truly need him.

I learned that although I lost his physical form (Earth suit) I have his living energy i.e. Soul or Spirit with me all the time.
And my pets are here too. It's the same principle of physics for all living energy.

The fact that you're reading my book indicates your Soul wants to evolve. Use what resonates to make choices.

Again, it's perfectly Ok to do things in your timeframe, in the way you feel and how you want to handle your going forward. However, to change things you have to **change you**. That's where your commitment begins.

Examine the Time You have on Earth

How old are you?
If you live to be 100 years old, your age is the percentage of life that you have already used up.
Age 65 equals 65% used and 35% left.
How do you want to live that last 35%?

Calculate how much life you have used
How much time do you have left to live?
Those numbers create real clear perspective.

Once you understand that all we really have is earth time to get this right, it makes going forward even more important. Deep breath, -Let's start!

Changing what you have and the situation that you are in, comes from changing who you are.

Changing who you are comes from changing what you think.

Changing what you think changes the consequences.

Recovery Starts in Your Mind

The greatest block to getting back on track is YOU thinking that it's impossible to do.

Never be a victim of your loss, even though it feels like that.

Your Choice is what determines your consequences.

It's been scientifically proven that there **is** a mind-body-spirit connection. "Mind over matter" is more than a catchy phrase. There is an entire field of medicine called mind body medicine due to the continuing documentation that your mind, emotions, body and spiritual connection affect and direct your healing and wellbeing.

You may "fake out" your friends with your "I'm trying" intentions; however, your mind and body will not be deceived!

You are the creator and selector of your thoughts." Those Choices (key word) affect and effect your life.

Lessons from Loved Ones in Heaven
How to Connect with your Loved One on the Other Side
to Heal from Loss

How to make Choices to Change Your Life

Free Will (Choice) is your greatest tool. "Free will" is a word phrase that means "do what you want to do." It's another way to state "choice." When you allow your free will to choose what you think, your thoughts become Choice. Thought choices determine how your body responds emotionally, physically, etc. to the mental decision you make.

Example: "That makes me sad," you feel/become glum and despondent.
"That makes me happy" and your mind focuses on good things.

Thought **choice**: "I'm not going to do anything." Doing nothing or staying at a standstill is a choice. "I'm going to learn to heal me." Your mind directs your body to find ways to get you better.

Choice **appears** simple. Free will is the mental action you must take to trigger your physical or mental thought process into reality, (i.e. "this is what I decide to think in order to do what I want to do.")

The hard part is creating and constructing each decision to control each thought (choice) that you want your mind, emotions and body to respond to. The movie *What the Bleep Do We Know *!?* illustrates a wonderful animated story that shows how your choice equals the consequence concept works.

Factually you command your free will (choice) breath-by-breath, minute-by-minute. You must "choose" a thought to create any activity. Even to do nothing **is** a choice!

Why am I starting with "choice" techniques? Because **choice is THE essence of life!** You choose to make the "choice" to heal, recover, reenter and create your life and new lifestyle.

Secondly, teaching the "choice" concept to children and others suffering from this scenario is one of the greatest gifts you can give them. By your example, everyone can learn that they are not a victim of loss and have the ability to choose how they want to live.

Choose How You Respond to Your Loss "Experience"

Why do I use the word "experience?" Experience means something that comes into your life and goes out of your life. It's only a **part** of your journey NOT a lifetime ongoing continuous event. Death and loss is a transition "experience" on your soul's path and evolution.

Learn to communicate using only the words "I choose to" or "it's my choice to."
Those words are the true essence of EVERY action, explanation, justification, excuse, emotion or eloquent presentation of what you "decide to do" in or with your life. They are some of the most powerful words on earth.

The choice perspective clarifies all intent of every emotion and action. When you strip everything down to "choice," it simplifies life.

By saying, "I choose," or "It is my choice," you are **choosing** to ACT, which is positive.
To choose to direct your mind is taking ownership of your personal power to do and be or live as you so choose.

"It's my choice." ensures that you will not be a "victim" of any situation especially a death event. You do not have to explain, justify, or give any reasons other than, **"It's my choice"** to use the tools you will be learning to recover from your loss.

IF you elect to tell someone why you made your choice that explanation is your gift to them. Otherwise it's your choice to say
"It's my choice!!!" Hopefully they will honor the methods that resonate with you to facilitate your recovery.

To ACT is to choose to direct and stand in your full power. You can't always choose what happens to you, but you can choose how you react to it.

To RE-Act is negative.
It makes you a victim of the loss and the circumstances surrounding the death. By reacting you give away your decision-making power to emotional responses about the death "situation." Having and choosing to honor your sad, angry, depressed, alone feelings is perfectly normal. It's part of the human grief process.

However, permanently RE acting to your loss with unending or extreme anguish and obsessive grief and mourning takes away your power of getting to make a choice in how your life will go forward.

How do you handle those normal reactive feelings then be able to move forward?

There will come a time, when you are tired of being sad, mad, unhappy and alone. If your reactions are ongoing for a long time. months and years, please seek professional help and counseling. Grieving is natural, unending suffering is not. Don't be ashamed. Asking for help is **positive** progress.

When you feel ready to readjust your
RE-Actions into Action, you'll be transforming the consequences of those feelings you've been choosing to allow to be in your life (i.e. sadness, depression, anger, guilt) and shapeshifting them into positive thoughts, actions and activities.
How do you do that?

You choose to ACT

ACTing **is a deliberate** choice using the power of your decision-making processes i.e. thoughts.

Choose to examine "what's the "learning opportunity" from your loss.
Ex. They are not in pain anymore.

Be the "what to be grateful for" student.
Ex: I was so fortunate to experience being loved by that person or pet.

Positive thoughts and Gratitude will feel like a hard choice. However, this thought choice process will prevent you from being an ongoing victim and start forward motion.

When do I do this Act/ choice thing?

Act Right Now

This is not the time to go on automatic pilot by reacting the way you've always responded to emotional issues and expect it will clear up. Grief will not "just go away." You have to choose to purge its consequences from you and your life by choosing to give yourself permission to live again.

You must be determined to direct your emotions and purposefully alter thought patterns and attitudes to have a positive outcome.

**Don't waste precious energy rehashing negative thoughts or emotions from your past. Those recollections whittle away your life and time on earth with each breath.

With each breath, your CHOICE is the greatest technique and tool to change.

Start now! You might want to put the statement above in a place where it will motivate you on an ongoing basis.

How do I stop those negative thoughts?

How to Change Negative Thoughts or Emotions into Positive

Science has found that you have about 20 seconds to cancel negative thoughts.
Your words have a ripple effect. That thought/choice begins an energetic change that creates a consequence. You can stop the ripple effect consequence within a 20 second timeframe.

Stop every negative notion whether you think it, say it, or find yourself in the presence of someone else who does something negative!

Here's how to do that. Say
"Cancel, Cancel, Cancel, next" |
That is the Negative Terminator Phrase.

The theory behind my "cancel, cancel, cancel" phrase is to transform negative emotions so they can't grow into an action during that 20 second timeframe and then create a consequence.

Use the following technique when you have a thought such as "I'm so sad."
Immediately stop that emotionally negative feeling from affecting you by declaring "cancel, cancel, cancel, next."

This phrase erects an energy shielding barrier that prevents you from emitting and absorbing any and even your own pessimistic energy. Subconsciously you may be helping those around you by illuminating their negativity as you're building this technique into your life.

CCC also erects an effective mental energy shield against absorbing any negative energy said or directed towards you from negative people or situations in your environment.

You might not always catch every negative idea that enters your mind. However, you **can** diffuse and negate them by thinking "cancel, cancel, cancel, next" in your mind or by speaking it outloud.

Why would you say "Cancel, cancel, cancel and add "next?"
"Next" creates a turning point that shifts your mind and energy in a new direction.
And then add "Positive!"
"Positive" redirects your thoughts into positive intention and action.

Collectively these statements reprogram the entire ripple effect and repel negative energy out of your mind, emotions, energy field and environment.

Ex: Someone says, "She is suffering from the loss of her husband or pet."
Deflect the negative energy conjured up by the word "suffering from" by replying out loud or in your mind.
"Cancel, cancel, cancel, next positive.

Instead say; "She's having a grief "experience."
Remember an "experience" comes and goes.

If you say "Next, Positive," out loud, most likely everyone in the room will ask you about this. Once they get this **turn around concept** they'll be more careful in constructing their communication around you.

"CANCEL, CANCEL, CANCEL, Next, Positive" is THE life changing phrase! You might want to display it so you can have a reminder. This phrase will definitely change things up and start discussions with those in your environment plus create a positive change in your life.

Self-Monitoring

The hard part of putting your new anti-negative shield in place is **relentless** self-monitoring. Monitoring will teach you how to recognize all the negativity and emotional downer thoughts that you need to reshape you.

Training yourself to make the "Cancel, cancel, cancel, next" phrase an automatic response will take about 3 weeks to accomplish.

Don't get disheartened in the early stages of reprogramming. Don't be upset when others discourage your efforts. You're standing in your power of choice and changing your interactions with the world. Standing in your power and truth will probably make other people uncomfortable learning how to interact with the new you. **That's their problem**. It's their learning opportunity and their choice of how to handle it.

The best technique is to practice this concept in small increments of time. Monitor yourself for just one morning, then one work day, then from morning to night. Most individuals discover that they are overwhelmed at how many negative thoughts, words, actions emotions and even people infiltrate their environment every day.

Take this inch by inch, don't backslide.
It will change the consequences in and the quality of your life! I suggest you use this phrase as your **permanent** monitoring technique to **insure** only "positive" anything is in your life.

My 90-year-old friend who has seen many of her dearest friends "pass on," after months of struggling to reprogram her old emotional responses, now walks around with a smile rather than as "an old growly bear." She says, "I'm doing that 'cancel, cancel next' and 'choice' thing."

She loves correcting her "not with it" nursing home friends. Her mission is to inspire everyone around her to live more positive despite all the challenges they face.

Quiz: How did your thoughts and choices affect your emotions and grief recovery today?

I'm not trying to be overly simple or tedious. It's imperative to master this concept and technique. Everything else going forward will be smoother because you'll be able to identify your thought choice glitches in order to reprogram and redirect your course of action.

"It's My Choice to…"

Here's how you proceed forward. "It's my choice" verbiage sets the tone for anything and everything about your healing recovery during your reentry back to life.

This phrase is a statement. It is not being defensive, judgmental, blaming, fake, manipulative, dramatic, emotional or has any hidden agendas.
This comment represents your Truth and your Power.

It validates how **you choose** to live your life.
THEN,
the other individuals have **their** choice of what to do with YOUR choice.

The loss of a person or pet in a family means individual relationship roles will change. Family members will need to talk, make new choices about the effects of this change and work out the shifts in responsibilities. These new choices and the consequences they make can be stressful for all the people or pets involved. Try to be even more gentle and patient when you are owning your new choices and others are having to get used to dealing with them.

If everyone in this loss experience would be this transparent about their choices, there would be greater understanding and no guessing or assuming. It would stop habitual negative energy games, toxic dramas and personal control tactics.

When you wake up each morning, it's the **first day of the rest of your life.**

Make every choice count! Your life is not spinning out of control. Teach everyone involved that what happens going forward is their choice.

The power of personal choice is like having an access pass to something amazing. I hope you choose to use it.

You've learned how to make Choices that
empower you to live as you choose.

Now let's learn what Death is and isn't.
It's a word I couldn't say for years
and now don't use
because
it's **not** factual.

Lessons from Loved Ones in Heaven
How to Connect with your Loved One on the Other Side
to Heal from Loss

Chapter 2- Understanding Physical Death
Transition

The fact that you are used to physical interactions from a Soul's earth suit is what creates human grief. It's a "you can see, feel, talk with and touch this" concept. One of the quickest ways to change the way you look at, perceive or believe about Death is to choose to use the word "transition" which is factual and the easiest way to change your thought process.

Transition is defined as the process or a period of time changing from one state (living energy on Earth) **to another.** (living energy called Spirit in Heaven, the Universe, or all there is etc.)

Here's a simple overview of the process;
A living Soul
discards their Earth Suit
transitions to Heaven, the Universe, Afterlife, the Other Side (there are lots of descriptive names for "all there is" i.e. the "Source")
where it becomes a living energy form called a Spirit!

Using the word Transition instead of Death, passed away, put down, or all the other denial words that are currently in style, states exactly what is happening.

Transition will shift your mind to the fact that their Soul's energy transitioned to the Other Side and is **still alive and well** in the place you think they go.

Transition is factually correct according to physics and is softer and gentler than "put down," put to sleep or euthanized if you are a pet lover. As you read further, you'll realize that "somewhere" is with and near you! And that will expand your awareness, reality and joy.

When you use "transition" around people, they will be curious about knowing why you choose that term. Subliminally, you will have opened a learning opportunity for their heart to consider. Before we learn more about the transition process, let's talk about a Memory Moment.

What is a Memory Moment?

It's a snapshot of a timeframe, activity, action or words that your heart will always recognize as "different" before the transition. FYI **all** beings on earth know when they will take or choose a particular exit point and leave, even if it seems like a sudden or accidental passing to you.

Before transition, at some point in time, your favorite person or pet will create a tender precious Memory Moment or a subtle announcement of what's about to happen. Sometimes you get both!

It's their way of acknowledging and honoring the love between you as they complete a lifetime. At first, during deep grief you might not recognize or be able to identify it. In hindsight, it will become a cherished and or vivid Memory Moment!

A Memory Moment is an action or behavior that is out of character for the way your person or pet or you normally behave or have been acting. (YouTube Video 22) Oftentimes I've heard people say, "it's as if he knew he was going to pass." That's the Universe alerting you that your contract is about to conclude.

Mike would **never** miss the Kentucky Derby. On Sunday before he transitioned we were driving home from the beach and he said. "I don't think I'll go to the Kentucky Derby this year." I yelled "what? You'd have to be dead for that to happen." It was my intuition giving me a preview of the future. I ignored what came out of my mouth.

Examples for pets are: one dog sat and stared deeply into it owner's eyes for several days before he passed. Another pet would lie on the other side of the terrace trying to distance her energy from their parents before she left. My Pet Life Radio.com show "Alive Again" has several great podcasts archived on this subject. Get your Kleenex ready.

A Memory Moment is also letting you know that everything is OK no matter what happens and that **they know** what's going on in reference to their impending departure!

Another loving pet example; a client's cat was extremely ill and stayed alone in a dark corner in her bed for months. Several days after the client started saying my Transition Affirmation, her cat got up, came over to sit in her lap and purred for the first time since her illness began. Later that night she calmly went to sleep (unassisted) in the safe haven of her owner's love while her guardian was stating that Affirmation. What a wonderful Memory Moment!

If you are in the presence of or aware that your beloved person or pet is preparing to leave, you can use this Transition Affirmation to bless their journey. Do not change the wording or it will change the type of energy sent.

Transition Affirmation:
"<u>Fill in blank with name</u>, I love you.
I honor, respect and support your choices.
From the love in my heart, I send you my life force energy to use as you so choose."

It is imperative that you use the words "as you so choose" so the person or pet can use that additional energy boost to gently cross over when they are ready to do so. Your words are honoring their choice and timing!

The week before Mike left, we spent a wonderful and romantic weekend celebrating the contract we put on our dream beach house. I was glowing.

The last words I ever said to Mike as he was preparing to drive back to his home in another state was "if you're tired next weekend, please take the train, because you'll get killed in that car." I thought it was strange that those words came out of my mouth. Little did my heart know how true that would become. That was Heaven whispering a heads up to me.

Always pay attention to what you say, especially if it was unexpected and out of context at that time. Sometimes your intuition and Heaven are giving you a heart alert Memory Moment that gives you a signal about what is going to occur.

FYI Never speak of your Spirit as a memory. i.e. "in memory of." The definition of a memory is "intended to remind people of, especially to honor a dead person."

Use "in celebration of" or "celebrating" instead. Spirit is not a recollection of the past dead person but a living energy!

A **Memory Moment** is a recall of a blip in time, not a living Soul.

Death is Transition to a New Life

What must I do to accept that my loved one gone? Learn that no Soul is ever gone.

As a reminder, everything is made up of energy. To have "life," any form, molecule or being must be inhabited by living electromagnetic energy which maintains a certain vibrational frequency in order for it to stay alive on earth. See YouTube video 228.

Physical death is the beginning of changing where your energy resides. When a Soul's energy vacates its earth suit it is immediately healthy, happy, whole and healed. It's ready to communicate and connect with you the nano second it vacates that body.

How do I know? As a Medium, I watch a Soul's energy transition and see them become Spirits on the Other Side. I use my Gift to help folks with questions about their beloved's transition.

Each biological body provides several opportunities (exit points) to separate the Soul's energy from the form it resides in. When the body ages, is physically broken or ill, just wears out or the Soul decides to opt out early during birth or the newborn process, it's the beginning of trading places from earth to Heaven!

**A Soul's energy NEVER dies,
it just changes forms!**

The durability of each body, its Karma (defined in Hinduism and Buddhism as the sum of a person's actions in this and previous states of existence, is viewed as deciding their fate in their future existences) and a Soul's contract choices determines each person or pet's physical life span.

Humans and animals have multiple exit points that they can choose to use to leave earth. That's why "when it's time," the person or pet inherently understands what's going on. It's a script you and your dearly departed, or you and your pet both agreed upon for this lifetime together.

No matter how gentle, sudden or horrific the transition is, remember, you both chose this specific scenario to enhance each Soul's growth.

Death is not "dead and done." Only the physical body has an expiration date. The Soul lives forever. Those facts help you understand the eternal cycle of life.

Here's an example that energy is never ending!
If you boil WATER, what does it make? STEAM
If you freeze STEAM, what does it become?

ICE CRYSTALS! If you melt ICE CRYSTALS, what does it become? WATER!

It's the law of physics! Energy never dies. Think about the water- ice- steam concept! The energy base of water never goes away; it just changes into different physical or energy forms.

Did you know that the human body is made up of about 75% water and a cat's body about 60%? According to the ASPCA, water makes up to 80 % of your dog's body weight.

Based on my example, I like to think of Mike and my pets in "steam" form. If you see deceased Spirits as I do, that Spirit energy looks like a see-through steam, sparkling fog, iridescent cloud or translucent glitter form of the original person or pet.

After arriving on the Other Side, all Souls transformed into a living energy called Spirit will now decide how they will continue their journey with you on Earth.

Some Spirits will choose to begin another earth lifetime with a new physical form. Choosing to inhabit another earth suit form is the process called Reincarnation.

The belief in Reincarnation and soul growth/ evolution through many lifetimes has been around for over 6,000 years and is embraced by the world's oldest and largest religion.

FYI, a Soul now in the Spirit realm will usually keep the same character traits, attitude and personality it had on earth!

However, if that Spirit returns to earth for another life, it may adopt new characteristics, genders and for animals, even different species. Example: a dog can come back as a cat, horse or bird, whatever is most appropriate for that next learning opportunity.

With people Spirits, the body is limited to male or female. Then they might add hair, skin tone, alter the body, ethnicity and other physical appearances, plus make new emotional or personality choices to try as a fresh experience for that particular life.

Are you still with me? Good!

The Progression of Transition

At the beginning of transition, a Soul's unending love for you will conflict with the earth body's selected exit point. Why? The Soul will want to stay on earth to emotionally and physically support you through his vacating that earth suit. However, every Soul understands that's not possible.

It's important for you to honor a Soul's choices of how to leave and their timing of when to leave. Release them to do and go "as they so choose"!

When a being is preparing to pass over and you subliminally want them to "hang on" for your sake, that Soul will walk away or distance themselves from you, not look at you in your eyes, avoid their normal personal contact habits, and pets will stay or hide in another room trying to avoid the conflicting energies.

Another sign of impending transition is when you see an older or sickly pet sitting at a window or door just staring out as if they are memorizing their last earthly view.
They are!

People also exemplify staring into the distance and talking about visiting with and talking to individuals on the Other Side, they are!! Hospice acknowledges that when this behavior begins, usually that individual departs within a 60 to 120-day window.

Now let's look at the 24 – 48 hours prior to leaving a body. The Soul will start to withdraw its life force energy from that earth suit. If you can see energy, their aura (defined as a field of subtle, luminous outside of the body radiation surrounding a person, pet or object like a halo) will gradually diminish and draw closer to the body instead of radiating outward as if did previously.

If you see Auras, you will be able to notice the Soul's electromagnetic life force energy (aura) becoming more centrally organized near the heart area. During that time, the physical body becomes colder as their energy is being incrementally withdrawn in preparation for departure. This progressive physical process starts as lackluster, glazed or nonresponsive eyes, cold limbs, pale gums, then shallow or intermittent breathing. Some healthcare professionals call these last hours of breathing for people and pets, the "death rattle" because it has such a distinctive cadence and signals the upcoming event.

You can also watch a Soul draw his life force energy **inside** of his body. As that process initiates, the body's exterior aura will begin to start getting lots of black holes in it. When the aura /energy surrounding the body becomes totally black, their Soul's life force energy has detached.

An interesting note- many end of life care nurses who don't watch energy professionally, report seeing a pale sheer cloud like, see through smoke form emanate from the earth body's shoulders and travel upwards into the heavens.

Disembodied energy then becomes whirling purple energy (that's THE highest Spiritual energy) as it rotates in an upward counter clock wise direction to cross over or transition over the death line, which is a solid black energy free area. Then that traveling energy will reappear on the Other Side as a bright white glittering sparkling steam form.

FYI, on earth, living energy is called a Soul. On the Other Side or in the Afterlife without a body, it's called a Spirit.

Remember this is a progression of changing places and spaces, **NOT a Dead end!**

I was always afraid of dying before I became aware of this earth to Spirit evolution. Since I am able to watch it, I'm not afraid anymore. It's just a zippy do da slip out of that outfit and you're fine!

Every meaningful Spirit being on the Other Side is with you before, during and after you swap forms.

It's important that I restate this fact,
a Soul **immediately** arrives in the Afterlife **perfectly whole, healthy, happy and healed** as a new Spirit.

There is no resting, waiting or adapting. They are ready to start a new journey with you RIGHT NOW!

"There will come a time when you believe everything is finished….
Yet
that will be the beginning."
Louis L'Amour

Lessons from Loved Ones in Heaven
How to Connect with your Loved One on the Other Side
to Heal from Loss

Chapter 3- Beginning a New Journey

The loss of an earth suit can NOT unravel, stop or impede never ending love. Choose to release old ideas of death with CCC, next and purge any limiting emotional blockages w CCC so you can experience validating that love is continuous, forever and always!

Death is a catalyst for change. You realize this when it impacts you. When you have reached the limits of your beliefs and they no longer serve you well, that's when you have a choice to grow.

No matter how you were born, raised and taught, or currently believe, I hope you will remain "open" to the following ideas so you can learn to receive, identify, validate and enjoy incredible gifts and experiences with your departed loved ones. They are forever and always near you!

You do not have to have any special talents, gifts or abilities. All you need to do is believe in your heart that your love connection is ongoing now, forever and always! What you are about to learn will prove this!

Everything in Heaven and on Earth is available to you after you get over the speed bump of your mind, open your heart's awareness, and trust your love connection.   **Let's begin!**

Spirits

We're not talking about ghosts or paranormal all things evil, that is marketed in the entertainment industry. Your religion will not throw you out nor ostracize you if you embrace the concept of Spirits. Nothing bad will happen if you show interest in, learn about and be aware of living energy.

Spirit is defined as an electromagnetic living energy who left its earth suit and now lives on the Other Side, Afterlife or Heaven. On earth that same living energy is considered a Soul and is called by its earth's body name like Mike or Fluffy. YouTube video 248.

A Soul's energy is what makes your EKG have an electromagnetic pattern and show up on the heart monitor. It's the same energy that is photographically captured on an MRI, CAT scan and X-ray. If it wasn't for a Soul's electromagnetic energy field, there would be no "alive" in your earth suit/ body.

Spirit lives on the Other Side. A lot of folks think there is a separate energy for humans and pets. **Energy is energy once it gets to the afterworld.** How you **remember** that energy's "earth suit" determines what form you think it is, a human or an animal.

An interesting note- don't let the earth suit fool you. There can be some very powerful and awesome beings' energy living inside. Do you know what we call an Angel is a form of electromagnetic energy? Earth people have assigned the name "Angel" to a specific frequency. Angels can inhabit an "earth suit" for their assignment to watch, guide or guard you.

Universal master teachers and Spirit Guides can also don the costume of a pet or person to facilitate their lessons for and with you. Your soul will have a really good idea that there's something very special behind those eyes! Some say my Mike was an Angel, other say their pet is an Angel. If a "special being" is wearing an earth suit, you and other people will feel a different presence when you are around them. And some may say, "there's something special about that person or pet." There is!

The techniques to communicate and connect with Spirit living energy whether pet or person is the same. My book **After Death Signs** focuses on pet and animal companions' life and has testimonials featuring animals.

Lessons from Loved Ones in Heaven focuses on the human transition process, and features techniques to communicate with **all** Spirit forms and a LOT more details for connection.

And speaking of Signs, I've had butterflies and Hummingbirds outside my window stopping and staring at me the entire time I was writing this book. Even several ladybugs stopped by. They obviously approve!

Lessons from Loved Ones in Heaven
How to Connect with your Loved One on the Other Side
to Heal from Loss

Why Connect with Spirit?

Now that you understand the Transition process, allowing Spirit into your life makes grief recovery quicker as you learn that "they" are not "gone". Grief tends to turn to joy as you become busy interacting with your special Spirit. YouTube video 235.

Spirit's view of "earth suit land" is life changing! You'll learn to see us from their perspective. Ask yourself "How would my beloved want me to grieve, recover and move forward?" Read a few more pages and you can ask Spirit yourself!

Connection with Spirit is different than Communication with Spirit and a lot of people think it's the same thing. Nope!

Why do I connect first? Although your special Spirit's energy will feel almost the same in either situation, once you've learned to identify a specific Spirit's energy pattern, then you are in control of who you interact with on the Other Side.

Connection with Spirit is based on electromagnetic energy exchanges.
It's based on pure energy, yours on earth and theirs on the Other Side. It's that magical connection of

the fibers of your heart's energy interwoven with their eternal living energy through Love.

While talking with Bobbie, Don and Spanky, we addressed a great question.
If you can't do one of the following techniques, does that mean you need to keep trying until you can? Or can you skip over it and move to the ones that you can do?

Some people will be able to do all connection techniques, others only a few. It depends upon your sensitivity to energy. Complete those that you can, skip over ones you're having trouble with and revisit them later.

You might get lots of Signs, but are unable to feel their hand or paw in yours. You can feel when they get in bed at night. or you might be able to see them out of the corner of your eye and have no dreams.

Why? Sometimes the connection you feel you need or want is **not** what Spirit wants to do or how they want to connect with you **at that time.** You may not get a lot of Signs because Spirit wants to focus on a closer energetic connection rather than just physical distractions. Spirit may also choose another form or interaction because they know you are ready for greater Soul growth.

Information about Connecting

How and when you connect is ultimately Spirit's choice.

Let go of those out dated perspectives that shackle you with grief and don't work. Give this new way to heal your heart a chance. Have faith.

When starting out, remember we each have different abilities for every lifetime. You'll learn what is comfortable and doable with your skill set.

It's best to set aside a specific time each day to contact Spirit because they are in "forever" infinity which has no time parameters. It's been proven that you will have a more consistent and productive connection if you initially schedule getting in touch with them about the same time every day.

I suggest being in a quiet space so you can focus better. You do NOT have to meditate, get in any "zones" or use any exterior enhancements like candles, music, darkness or whatever to prepare for these exercises.

I prefer to do these barefooted (or in socks) because it is more grounding (and warmer) for me. You can keep your shoes on if that's your preference.

Lessons from Loved Ones in Heaven
How to Connect with your Loved One on the Other Side
to Heal from Loss

Normally it takes about 2 weeks to have an "on demand" response. Reconnecting with your beloved reignites your heart light that was dimmed by loss. It also rekindles your will to live again. Connection with Spirit begins your journey back to living again.

How many times have you awakened during the middle of the night in the early morning hours to see numbers like 3:33. 5:15, 4:45 etc., hear subliminal sounds or voices, see something out of the corner of your eye, get smells or experience a distinct feeling that you feel a presence in the room, next or near to you. Bet it's during those hours.

According to research, the best time to receive Spirit connection and communication is between 11 pm and 6 am in the United States on the east coast. You can apply this same time to your local time zone when you understand the principle behind it.

Usually by 11 pm most electronic equipment in our east coast area is shutting down and doesn't start up until 5:30 to 6 am. Those hours have the least amount of interference from earth energy emissions. That time frame is a quiet open window. With less obstacles, Spirits can get through to you better.
FYI, many creative people who channel music, art, books, etc., work late into the night and into the wee morning hours because they can best receive and hear their guidance more clearly during that time.

How to Connect with Spirit

The following is not a class in mediumship, psychic reading, gypsy mediation or animal communication. It's not a séance, crystal or mirrored ball class nor something "woo woo." These are specific techniques for you to connect with **your** Spirit, not others, **just yours**! It's an investment into eternity. Why? No matter where you are, in what form, you'll always be together.

If you're not the do it yourself type, there are other methods. Psychic readings, psychic medium sessions, animal communication and animal medium readings are a way to derive information from Spirit for peace of mind and get some tidbits in addition to the information you receive.

Before you start any connection or communication you might want to ask yourself the questions below:
*Are you being obsessive about contacting because you feel you can't move on?
*Are you SO upset and consumed by sorrow that you are unrealistically lonely?
*Are you so co-dependent on your relationship that you can't let go and allow your Soul to evolve with the lessons you learned and shared?

If so, there is a time to seek awareness and a time to move forward. Please go to grief counseling if necessary. Prolonged emotional "I can't get over this" attitudes and I want to "be with them" are unhealthy and require professional help.

An "I can't let go- dead end" attitude dishonors all the joy and love you unconditionally shared. Spirit wants you to be happy! That's why they are in your life in the first place. Just because they vacated their earth suit does NOT stop them from sharing joy and happiness with you in another form. **Only your mind's choices can stop t**hem from being a part of your ongoing life.

You choose the attitude to celebrate what you **have now** on this new journey together or cause the transition relationship to be a septic tank of sadness!

Think about it, Spirits can be with and around you 24/7/365, waiting to connect and communicate **all the time**, EVERYWHERE! They are free to go anywhere, anytime with no restrictions other than your beliefs and choices.

After Mike's transition, he stayed with me during those early years. Then his visits became less frequent because I was less needy for him as I recovered and moved forward.

People always want to know where do they go and who are they with? When a pet or person sheds it earth suit it goes back to the original energy source that we call God, Heaven, the Universe, "all there is" or your preferred name for that space. All energy lives in that space. Your Spirit is with every pet or person that is in now in energy form. YouTube video 228 help explain.

The other most asked question is "who is taking care of them?" With no body, there is no need to be taken care of. Continuing your Soul to Soul connection is the highest way you can honor your beloved and never-ending relationship.

What if you didn't get along with and didn't like the departed Soul? In that case, you can use these exercises to get answers, have lengthy discussions to work out your Karma and move forward with understanding.

Although Mike recognizes I've grown beyond requiring his presence all the time, 20+ years later he's still and **always** with me for special occasions, emotional support/opinions/ decisions or protection.

You're now moving into another wonderful chapter of sharing **unless** YOU allow the following disruptions.

What interferes with Connection?

Personal choices, emotional and mental filters can diminish, delay and restrict Spirit's eagerness to connect.

Memorial spaces can be negative because they're a constant reminder of "the death" and what a pet or person "used to be!"

IF a griever goes to a specific memorialization and predetermines a connection with Spirit can **only** be made thru that "memorial" form.   WRONG- This is a limiting mindset.

Photos in a frame saying, "I'll be waiting for you." Why? That mentality erodes the reality of Spirit's availability right NOW!

If you believe erroneous facts, that can be limiting. If anyone tells you
"Spirit is staying around because you need them to" or "not crossing over" or "not moving on" because you miss them so much or "busy on the Other Side" or "has to wait to be healed" or "is tired" so they can't connect with you is WRONG!

Excessive grief, anger, depression, isolation and lack of faith in your ability can also block connection progression as we mentioned in various chapters.

Most Important

Some people are fearful of connecting with Spirit because they were taught it's a bad thing, or are made afraid by ingrained beliefs or read something negative. Others just don't want to "go there" because they don't feel safe or were told it's evil and your friends will think you are crazy.

Others are caught up in the media hype drama of negative sensationalism which is wrong. Spirits send Signs and Visit because they want you to be comforted, happy and have clarity for your new life plus still continue with you, just in a different way.

If you're like me, it's more important to gather courage and reach out to your beloved to find out and validate what is **really** going on! The reward for a believer is ongoing never-ending love and a higher understanding of the cycle of Life.

How to protect yourself before you begin any contact with the Other Side.

Why do I need this? When you open a connection to the Spirit world, you **only** want your Spirit to respond. Be **very specific** so you won't open a portal for any and all energies and entities that want to connect and share their story with you or someone else on Earth.

Protection = correct and specific wording!

How to Pray
Be SPECIFIC!

Spirits live in "forever time" and your earth suit/body lives in finite time, so you need to be **very specific** about what you want from Spirit. Please read that again.

Start with I ASK, "ask and ye shall receive." It's a Universal Law that all those in charge of your soul's contract must respond. You're asking all those in charge of your soul to help you, now! Why not use all the powers you have on heaven and earth that are available to you?

It is MY INTENT (with a "T" NOT Intend with a D) that brings your prayers into the **now,** in this incarnation, at this very moment in time.
You **must be very specific!!!!!!!!!!!!!!**

Be VERY specific about **exactly what you want** and in a VERY SPECIFIC timeframe. Not being specific (intend) is never never land, or "which incarnation?" etc. to those on the Other Side.

I suggest that you say your prayer 3 times.
3 is the universal number.
*The first time sets your free will to ask for help,
*the second time your prayer creates intent
*the third time to me, means you're really focused on getting this accomplished!

Use the words **Now, Forevermore and Always**.

"Now," brings your prayer into the present. For Them to respond to your command you must state "now", otherwise your Guides and Spirits will be asking " when do you want this done?"

"Forevermore," takes the prayer into all energy realms, incarnations and time frames. **"Always,"** makes the prayer request continuous with no lapses.

At the finale of your request **Say: So be it, it is done. Thank you.**
"So be it," brings the prayer into your present situation. **"It is done,"** makes the prayer a reality, NOW!

Although not necessary, I take off my shoes and say my Protection Prayer.

****

Protection Prayer: (YouTube video 53)

I ask and it is my intent, to surround myself in a seamless mirrored--(bubble or cocoon) of the Christ White Light (or whomever is your Higher Power), to protect me now, forevermore and always. Only allow the energy or entities which are for my soul's highest and best good to come thru. So be it, it is done. Thank you.

This is THE prayer to say at **any** time in **any** place, whenever you want to protect yourself from any and all energies and entities!

Why do I use the words **seamless and mirrored?** Seamless means nothing comes in or out of your being's energy field or environment unless you allow it.

The concept of mirrored means that any negative energy or entity, event or whatever that is aimed at you, **reflects back** to the sender so that you will not be drained or affected. SO, easy!

*** If you change the wording of a prayer you will receive different results. ***

Next, **ask Spirit permission** to contact and work with them either out loud or telepathically with your mind or heart.

You will hear the answer in your inner consciousness.

NOW You are ready to request Spirit to send Signs, come to visit, contact or energetically connect with you.

*** A MAJOR mistake **that causes disconnection** and all sorts of problems-is- Do NOT use IntenD use **INTENT!**

Chapter 4- How to Connect with Your Loved One

Types of Spirit Connection

You have the tools, you **can** do this!

1. Signs. Spirits use their electromagnetic energy field to create or manipulate a Sign for or around you.

2. Touching and Feeling Spirit. You can heighten the nerve sensitivity in your hands in order to feel your own, others or Spirit's energy. My Mother's Garden club all 86 years or older could do this, so I bet you can too!

3. Sharing space with Spirits involves another more heighten sensitivity.

4. Spirit sounds are maneuvered to get your attention. Examples: Slamming a door, rattling a food bowl, bark, meow, neigh or chirp, footsteps on the floor.

5. Smelling Spirit
You can't see this connection however the olfactory sensation is energy that you recognize and identify with your sense of smell. Examples: Their favorite cigar, fragrance, sweat, wet dog smell or fur.

6. Dreams are in between connection and communication. It's a Sign, an energy emotional feeling that originates in your mind and a visual appearance of your Spirit all at one time.

7. Seeing Spirit from glimpses in sparkler form to full blown visitations.

8. Orbs are a specific circular shape used by Spirit for a social call to visit with you.

Signs from the Afterlife & Other Side

Pets and people want to let you know that they are alive and well and **still** with or near you. They usually begin by sending simple Signs.

Signs are a form of show and tell communication defined as "means of connection between people or places" as in this instance, from your Spirit on the Other Side.

Signs are electromagnetically constructed and manipulated to get your attention. Example: feathers, flickering lights, molecular cloud formations, phone and doorbell rings, computer glitches, oversouling and many more.

Signs are how Spirits subtlety start the process of revealing to you they are a continuing and integral part of your daily routine.

At first, it's normal to doubt Signs. Why? If you're not aware of nor embracing the concept of living Spirits, you think "how can this be true?" It is!

Once you give Spirit a little encouragement, they will display more and more Signs until you become more comfortable with the fact that it's real. 21years later Mike's Signs are still going strong.

Signs are **not** affected by how long a person or pet has been gone. The quality and quantity of Signs that you receive are **not** affected by time either.

Signs are the ongoing reminder that Love is never ending and your connection continues with or without a body. Oftentimes you get a "kick in the butt" OMG Sign that there is **no way** you could miss it. Then you realize it's a Sign for **you** and your life is changed forever!

Being open to and receiving that life changing awareness also alters how you view future transitions!

Choose to encourage your Spirit to stay in touch on an ongoing basis.

How Spirits decide What Signs to Send

Although it's always important to listen to your inner guidance, sometimes your dearly departed will redirect your routine for you to find a special message.
That's a favorite trick to get you to focus on their message. They'll lead you astray and then voila, a Sign!

Think about it. Spirits don't know when you are going to ask for a Sign. They are required to consider and coordinate a lot of factors. They need to determine where you are and when, and how they will send **the** Sign that will mean the most to you. They also wonder if you will listen to their subliminal suggestions to see, feel, hear or experience that Sign, or brush it off.

Spirits are VERY innovative and persistent in unimaginable, **to the max**, ways! Just ask. Allow Spirit to choose how, what, where and when to deliver the Signs. You will get more and it will be worth any wait! They like showing off how much they care!

TRUST your Spirit's creative choice and timing. If you have trouble identifying a signal or are confused and think "could it be," ask yourself, "how often has this occurred before?" Most likely, never. That fact confirms it's a Sign.

Don't doubt, second guess or question their ability to send and **your ability to receive**. Be thrilled! What a Gift!

NO, you are not crazy!!! You are aware of "all there is!"

Usually Signs come when you are relaxed with no expectations. Try to make a quiet time each day and ask to be contacted then. Some people like to visualize scenarios that they want. Personally, I prefer specific requests, so there is NO confusion about what I am asking for and when I'd like to have a response.

Did you know you can get Signs **during or immediately after** Transition?

Is asking for Signs immediately after Transition OK? Yes. Some people erroneously think you must wait while Spirits heal, rest, or adjust when they get to the Other Side. WRONG.

Spirit is IMMEDIATELY ready to connect with you! Don't require them to sit around waiting for you to get ready for them. What do I mean by that?

Spirits will honor **your** free will choice. If you are afraid of receiving a Sign they will wait until you give them permission to do so.
If you choose to believe Spirit can't send Signs, they won't. Doubt or disbelief is a huge factor in having little or no Signs.

Not everyone has a place to ask questions or learn more about these subjects. You're invited to join my Facebook Groups where we discuss transition, Signs, communication, techniques, frustrations and much more.

I want you to have a safe factual, uplifting support system and a haven for your heart where you are welcome to share your dilemmas and experiences with Spirit.

for People:
Missing Loved Ones in Heaven & Afterlife- in Loving Memory

for Pets:
Animal Life after Death, Pet Loss, Afterlife Sign, Reincarnation <3 Answers

And join our LIVE discussions and Events on Brent Atwater Live Page.

Excessive Grief Affects Signs

If you are reading this book immediately after the transition of your loved one, don't get SO angry or frustrated that you can't hear or receive the Signs you want. If you're having trouble with the connection techniques, just keep trying and talk with others in the same boat. Our group discussions will help you reach your goals.

Although part of the natural emotional process, **extreme** or prolonged grief or anger will interfere with your ability to receive anything from Spirit. Once your emotions are less intense, revisit the techniques and you will be able to do them with a little practice.

For the initial outcome, have no expectations which is hard to do in highly emotional times. It's about mutual love and respect.

Again, it takes about 2 weeks to regularly connect with the Other Side **on demand**." This does NOT mean that you must wait that long.

Your beloved companion is interwoven into the fabric of your being, so chronic sobbing pushes energy away. Negative crying pulsates in a vibrational direction that repels energy from your body)))))))))))))). It creates a barrier and hampers

Spirit's ability to connect with you in the best way possible!

What is negative crying? Ranting, raving, pleading, begging or yelling like I did at the Universe, aren't expressions of hospitality and don't offer a warm welcoming- "come on in" door for Spirit.

Negative crying also comes from being resentful after loss, angry about why this is happening to me, possibly from over medication, or a "dead is gone" mentality, or from a codependent earth suit unfulfilled neediness. They are "my everything," I **can't move** on is negative.

Positive crying comes from your soul being triggered by a heartfelt memory, thoughtful occasion and a touching environmental, sound, smell or scenario. It's a grateful or celebratory recognition of your love. YouTube video 10.

Lessons from Loved Ones in Heaven
How to Connect with your Loved One on the Other Side
to Heal from Loss

How to Ask for Signs

Protect yourself at the beginning of each day or BEFORE you start each Prayer or Request.

When ready say
I ask and it is my intent to contact (my person or pet previously called) _____. I ask _____ to send me a Sign that I can easily recognize and understand within the next hour or ____ days to tell me what he wants me to know. So be it, it is done, Thank you (name).

Signs are normally very clear and distinct. Your heart WILL recognize and KNOW it's them! If you wonder and think "it might be,"
it most likely IS!!

Spirits always send the most appropriate Sign that will touch your heart to heal your grief in the most perfect way and timing. There are NO coincidences.

IF you want to know **which Spirit** is sending **a particular Sign**, use the prayer below.

Prayer to ask if Sign was sent by Spirit
"Mike or Fluffy (insert name)
I ask you to tell me NOW,
did you send the Ladybug as a Sign today, Yes or No?"

Or you can say
Which Spirit sent me the _____ today?
Tell me the answer now. So be it, it is done.

I ask 3 times to create clear intent and focus. You'll hear the answer in your heart or mind.

How do I know it's not me answering myself?
(YouTube video 51 and 109)
Answers from Spirit will usually come instantaneously, i.e. the **immediate** response you hear.
If your answer presents slowly, it's probably your mind doing a quick analysis and answering you.

* **Most important!** As you begin these techniques, if you can't do one, say "I can't do this **YET**!" That statement leaves the door open for you being able to do the exercise at a later time. Then move to the next one.

How to Touch & Feel Spirit Energy
(YouTube video 20 and 203)

What's the importance of this exercise?
Once you have learned to identify, connect and validate your interaction with a **specific** Spirit then you will be more "in tune" with the Signs they send or when they Visit. The energy of the earth suit and the Spirit will feel about the same however with no body, the Spirit energy may feel stronger.

What is the step by step guide for this technique?
I say the Protection prayer each morning to cover my day, before each reading and before each request to Spirit. Do what resonates with you. I'd rather be overprotected than not. I also only say the protection prayer once. Use the exact words and you'll be completely safe!

****** The hand that you do **NOT** write with is **your "receiving energy" hand**.
If you are right handed, then your left hand is your receiving hand. Use the receiving hand, wrist, etc. as the place where you want Spirit to touch you.

While standing or sitting, rub the palms of your hands together until they feel warm. When your palms are warm they have been "sensitized to feel energy." Then face your receiving hand palm upward to the ceiling and Say,

I ask and it is my intent to contact name _____,
so I can feel _____ here NOW.
I ask _____ to put your (hand, paw, lips whatever) into or on my _____ (hand, face) NOW.
(you can substitute where you want them to put their energy like on my left thigh, foot, or face. It **must be** on your receiving hand side.)
So be it. It is done. Thank you.

If this doesn't work at first, then rub your hands together again to re-sensitize them and start the process again. Most people feel "something" by the 3-5th try. The reason you may not "feel" immediately is because you are acquainting yourself with a new way to interface with their energy.

Being specific with the name ensures that you connect with the **exact** Spirit you choose in the exact location you want. Don't worry. You won't get any strange, scary or dangerous responses.

If you're uncomfortable feeling/ sensing/ recognizing and validating their energetic presence, use the prayer for asking to see them in your dreams in a later chapter.

If you are extremely emotional or uncomfortable you might not be able to sense/ feel / recognize Spirit's energy at first. Take the time to calm down! Trust!

This method works! My Mother's 86-year-old Garden Club members could do this.

In this exercise, you are learning how to recognize/identify and validate a specific energy "presence." Everyone gets different responses. You may feel tingles or pulsating in your hand, "thick weighty" air, a sense of pressure or cold or maybe a warm air area **that is different from the surrounding air**, or like pressing on a balloon. It's subtle and its real!

It's also normal to sense your beloved sometimes as a warm sensation and other times as a cold sensation because of the area of your body they are touching or the environment you are in.

NO, you are NOT crazy! You have now felt and identified the Spirit that you called in. You have experienced and felt their **specific** and **individual** energy pattern. Every Spirit has a unique blueprint.

You can practice this by having a person use their sending hand (i.e. the one that they write with) to touch your energy field. FYI kids love this game, and are quite good at it because they are so open minded.

Stand 4 feet apart facing each other. Both people rub your hands together to sensitize your hands. Have the sending person hold their sending hand palm facing your receiving hand palm about 3 feet away.

Ask them to slowly bring their open palmed sending hand toward your open palmed receiving hand until you can sense and identify a different feel of the air between the two of you. Your palm may register a sensation like you've bumped into a thicker air, or tingle, or feel cool or pushed away. When you have "bumped" into each other, you have connected to and are in their specific energy field.

If it doesn't work at first, try again. This is simply a matter of you getting accustomed and sensitive to energy of a practice person or from the Other Side. Learning energy identification is a requirement for any tactile contact with the Other Side or anyone who works with Energy.

If it works the first time and then not again, ask yourself what are **you** doing to block the exchange of energy.
If you did it once, you have the ability to always do it again!

Can I do these techniques with any person or pet Spirit that I lost even years ago? Yes! Every Spirit, like a snowflake has a unique energy signature pattern that you can learn to identify when you ask that specific Spirit to show up. Once you've identified their individual frequency pattern whether, Grandpa, Mother, Sister, Husband, Partner or Pet, **it is always accessible.**

Again, it's best to specifically invite only one Spirit at a time to visit.

Remember, usually it takes up to 2 weeks before Spirit will show up "on demand" because they're running around with no timeframe. Practicing the techniques about 30 minutes each day will accelerate your abilities. Go to the next technique whenever you choose.

Now that Spirit is visiting me when I request them, what do I do? Enjoy your new awareness about after death connection!

If I contact my Spirit, am I interrupting him from whatever he is supposed to be doing on the Other Side?
NO! Why would he be busy with anything else? His connection is with **you** all the time until you feel secure! However, being impatient can and will delay your request's response. Impatience is a prickly type energy and vibrationally pushes outside energy away. How much do you like being around an impatient person? See what I mean?

As times passes and you become less emotionally dependent, Spirit will hang out with other Spirits in "all there is," until you request or require their presence. Then snap they're there!

Of note- sometimes extreme eagerness to receive instant gratification through an immediate response is an issue stemming from grief. Trust that their timing will be perfect.

FYI- Spirit will also just "show up" at times to "check on you" or just to let you know they're OK. Enjoy the Gift!

Sharing Space with Spirits

Since you'll be interacting more fully with a Spirit's presence rather than just on your hand, here's more information.

Spirit energy can cause the temperature in the room to drop, that's why oftentimes people feels chills around a so called "ghost" energy. Usually cold energy means there's a close Spirit presence, but not necessarily something to be afraid of. See YouTube video 71.

Every night of my life, all 3 dogs slept on my bed in their special spots. After Mike's death, I would go to bed wailing, screaming and crying for him.

I thought I perceived a little bump and a weight jousting the bed like a person climbing in next to me. I would blow it off as imagination and go back to crying and pleading with Heaven to bring back Mike.

I also felt a cool air feeling and slight tingling on my right side each night but wrote that off too. I thought I was probably hyper ventilating to explain the tingling and me being so tired to explain the "cold" I felt because I wasn't sleeping.

As these events began to occur, each dog would carefully, with their head down and tail tucked, quietly sneak off the bed and go lay down on the floor surrounding my bed and stare at the bed or ceiling.

For years I ignored this nightly incidence.
I was totally unconscious and unaware as to what was happening. I was so caught up in my grief and had such a closed mind that I missed out on being able to share a beautiful connection. Mike was sleeping beside me every night.

Before Mike's transition, I did not know interacting with living energy/ Spirit on the Other Side was even possible! I'd heard about it, but blew it off as "airy Fairy." Plus, being raised as a Christian, I was afraid to be involved in anything "like that!"

Many years later when I was less skeptical and beginning to be receptive to new ideas and concepts about the Other Side, Mike patiently instructed me on how to do these interactive techniques.

After I learned how to recognize and validate the presence of his specific Spirit, we would hold hands and he would hug and kiss me every night before I went to sleep. His Spirit still sleeps beside me years after he has vacated his biological being.

Even now, my "B" bottom Friend, looks up at the ceiling every night as he leaves the pillow and goes to his special bed on the floor. I feel safe and content knowing I'm not sleeping alone!

Growing up I always heard that "God is Love." Through my experiences with Mike's after death connection and communication, plus learning these techniques **from him**, I totally understand love transcends everything and is everlasting!

I **know** beyond a shadow of a doubt that a Soul's energy and love is forever and always, alive and well and NEVER ending!

As a client said, "it's nirvana to touch a Spirit rather than just talking to it, it's life changing!"

Now let's meet your favorite Spirit!

Lessons from Loved Ones in Heaven
How to Connect with your Loved One on the Other Side
to Heal from Loss

Being with Spirit "on demand"

Here's how you ask for greater interaction, say
I ask and it's my intent for <u>name</u> Spirit to Visit me NOW.
I ask _____ to visit me NOW
I ask _____ to visit me NOW
I ask _ to visit me NOW SO be it, it is done.
Thank you _____.

How do I confirm my Spirit has "showed up?"
Use the earlier presence recognition exercise to have them put their energy in your hand. Once a specific Spirit will do that on a regular basis, then use the prayer above and follow the instructions below.

Now that Spirit has "shown up," and you can identify the feel of their specific energy pattern, let's learn how to connect with them on an ongoing basis.

1. Rub your hands together until they are warm to activate the nerve endings in your palms and fingertips so you can sense energy to the "max."
If you need to "refresh" your sensory sensitivity, just do this "warming up" exercise and start over as many times as necessary.

2. Spread your fingers apart with about **at least** a half inch of space between each finger, like a wide toothed comb. That increases your sensitivity to

feeling energy. Don't have stiff fingers! Bend them slightly like the top of a C although spread apart in a relaxed manner.

3. Very SOFTLY, as if you are trying to touch the dust on butterfly wings, start SLOWLY sweeping your hands horizontally back and forth within about a 4-foot-wide path and within a 4-foot-high rectangular area in the vicinity you sense your Spirit is located.

Continuously scan for their energy back and forth left to right or vice versa and top to bottom through the space you think they are inhabiting. (YouTube Video 21 and 203)

Keep working in rectangular quadrants until you feel and or sense "something" in the manner that your body registers/ receives energy input.

As previously described, Spirit can feel like a thicker, puffier, denser, usually cooler area or a section that causes your hand to tingle. It can also feel like "fat air," a warm balloon or like two magnets pushing against your hands in a large area. That's your Spirit's energy field! Your heart will **know** it's them!

The softer and more consistent your movements are and the slower (i.e. don't rush this) you approach any energy field, the greater the sensory input you receive.

Don't be so fearful or doubtful that you brush off reality!

Be patient and practice, practice, practice! This will allow your tactile recognition of various and specific Spirits to occur more rapidly. Don't get frustrated, in time, this works.

You can ask them to come play and stay! Now, you and your Spirit can interact together for the rest of your life on Earth to continue your never-ending love story!

Being "sensitive to a different feel of air space" is how you progress. When you get good at this, you can learn to feel the distinct edges of their Heavenly form.

When you get really good, you can be aware of and feel them walking on your pillow, getting in your lap or sleeping beside you. Perhaps, holding your hand, kissing your lips and lots more!

A friend shared this "last night after I experienced the chill over the left side of my head, I turned off the TV, rolled over on my right side, and told my beloved good night and that I love him, like I always do, I got the chill again. Only on the left side but this time it started on the head and slowly went down only my left side. I literally had goose bumps only on my left side from head to toe. I have never had this happen before! But I pray that it's him and he's showing me that he is with me and that he loves me still."

That's a wonderful account of how a sleep over with Spirit can occur.

The following may be the most unusual paragraph for those who have never heard of this. It will be confirming information for those who have experienced sex with Spirits.

A friend's Grandmother used to say that Grandpa would visit and they would make love all night long and she was just beaming the next morning as she related what had gone on. I reacted in shock.

Then several credible individuals talked about having similar experiences. Others relayed enjoying sensual and sexual activities in their dream states. I decided to research this concept and to have an in-depth conversation with Mike to get even more insight from the Other Side.!

Factually, it's electromagnetic energy that stimulates your nerves which create the sensations that you enjoy in physical encounters of the closest kind. And its electromagnetic vibrations that create responses in your physical body like wet dreams etc. Use your imagination. Perhaps the movie *Ghost* illuminated some accurate observations.
Form your own conclusions.

Lessons from Loved Ones in Heaven
How to Connect with your Loved One on the Other Side
to Heal from Loss

Dreams

A Dream embodies the states of feeling energy, experiencing interaction with their presence, telepathic connection, auditory and olfactory recognition and seeing spirit visitations. It's a concentrated combination of any or all of the above because you can sense odors, sounds, feelings, physical sensation and manifestations plus lots more.

Many individuals want to have dreams visits with communication because they feel it's safer and more intimate. All methods are safe with the Protection prayer. Why? Because all of these techniques are honored by your Spirit's heart connection to you.

Some dreams are so real that you feel what's going on. Others so profound that you wake up, go to the bathroom or get a drink of water and then go back to sleep and rejoin where you were in the origin dream. It's as if you hit a pause button on the dream control.

Many folks have mini visions in a semi-conscious state just before falling asleep or in the early morning hours before awakening. A lot of people call that consciousness the dream state. Why?

At that time, your body is more relaxed, quiet, and you are more receptive to interrelating with Spirit. Your mind is not cluttered with lots of busy thoughts, bereft with grieving emotions and bombarded by external environmental input.

Some Spirits prefer to use dreams, others don't like that contact method at all. Don't get depressed if your favorite Spirit doesn't choose this form of communication with you.

IF your friends and parents get dreams, you should not feel left out. That's just your Spirit's way of providing a backup confirmation that they are letting you know they are alive and well.

Have you noticed that when a Spirit wakes you up in or from a dream, it's from the inside emotional connection of your heart and soul. That's where the dream connection originates.

Can you have dreams of your pet or person passing or premonitions of the events before their transition? Yes.

Can you be forewarned of what you may go through with them in the future? Yes!

Usually bad dreams reflect the interpretation and fears of your current emotions. Before you get all upset about a specific dream that you may have replayed several times, examine your emotions and negative thoughts to see if they contributed to the dream's script.

Our Facebook groups and radio shows also have dream interpretation guidance to help you sort out the message. Don't be afraid to ask!

Dreams area a powerful connection and communication tool. There are many wonderful reference books about dreams and more information that can be found on the internet.

Lessons from Loved Ones in Heaven
How to Connect with your Loved One on the Other Side
to Heal from Loss

How to Ask Spirit to Visit in Dreams

Say:
I ask and it is my intent to contact (person or pet) previously called _____.
I ask _____ to visit me in my dreams tonight or during my nap or _____. I ask _____ to show me what he wants me to know in a way that I can easily understand and will remember. So be it, it is done, Thank you!

FYI- Practice about 30 minutes a day or whatever feels comfortable for you. It works!

If you want Spirit to answer questions in your dreams, again, be VERY specific about what you are requesting. Remember, Spirit will answer when they so choose.

How soon after transition can I use any of these techniques?

Immediately is fine! There are **no** time constraints for contacting a deceased loved one.

How to Ask a Specific Question in a Dream

Use the Spirit's earth name. Ask only one specific question at a time. Say

I ask and it is my intent to contact (person or pet) previously called _____. I ask _____ to visit me in my dreams tonight or during my nap or_____. (Timeframe like within 48 hours)
I ask _____ to show and or tell me the answer to the following question in a way that I can easily understand and will remember.
Name, Why do you_____or
Are you made at me or _____.
So be it, it is done, Thank you!

I kept a notebook of Mike's answers. When feeling sad or lonely I'd go back and revisit his messages to me. You might want to keep a journal of answers, dreams and visits. Many years later it will still be an educational and interesting read!

Oftentimes a person will say prayer requests for a period of time and have no results. Sometimes it's not the correct timing for you to know **that** answer. Otherwise, if no answer is the case, ask again! Usually the person posing the question did not use **specific** verbiage and "changed up" or threw in a "few of my own words" in the format of my request. That will not work. There is a reason for each word.

I've spent 20+ years crafting these prayers to manifest positive results!

Also, your grief may be so strong that it's interfering with receiving any or correct answers. Trust Spirit will reply in perfect timing. Doubting prevents Them from completing your requests.

Even with great dreams, some people want more, more, more! That's doable! Let's go there!

Lessons from Loved Ones in Heaven
How to Connect with your Loved One on the Other Side
to Heal from Loss

Stronger Spirit Connections

Craving more connections other than Signs, touching your beloved and having great dreams is perfectly understandable. To me, it's like delicious chocolate, you just want more!

To have more, you don't have to believe in anything. You need to have confidence in the heart connection you shared. It's a **knowing** rather than a "is this really possible" mentality. If you're still unsure, then practice until you prove it to yourself.

The more you experience Spirits and how they can communicate and connect with you on a daily basis, then the separatism surrounding death doesn't become as important. Spirit presence becomes your new tangible instead of the earth suit. That's when you realize there is no separation.

Shopping sprees with Mike are a constant example. I can be looking at a flowery shirt and Mike will comment "don't buy that blouse, it will draw bees." So, I return it to the rack and we go onward! Or I can look across a crowded room and he'll be there with his endearing smile that melts my heart. Whew!

In normal everyday living you don't look for or expect a visual appearance from Spirit. However, if you really want to see Spirit and you **have the**

ability to see energy (key) in this lifetime, when the student is ready for a visitation, Spirit gladly appears.

Let's get started!

Types of Visitation

1. Energy Presence (YouTube video 20) An Energy presence occurs when you sense/ feel and recognize their presence but do not actually see it. It's a beginning energy connection. It's in the seeing Spirits category because it's like the bud before the flower. It has a closed form, but you know the flower is inside.

Typically, if you can feel or sense a strong energy presence from your special Spirit, their next entrance is usually the quickie Sparkler form.

After spending the nights with me, Mike would stand behind or breeze past me just to get my attention and to acclimate me to his presence. Then one night he began to materialize by starting in a disorganized splattered glitter format that was slowly transforming and reconfiguring into his human likeness.

I panicked and told him to stop because I was afraid and would have a heart attack if he was full form. My greatest regret is that I asked him not to show up when he wanted to. He honored my request and over 20 years later only appears sporadically. Why don't I want to fully see him and reach for him and talk with him? Because I would desperately want to hug him and be held. It makes me sad to be able to see thru his form!

I'd rather interact with him every day in a touchy feely way and not see what I'm missing. It's easier for my mind to handle.

2. Glitter or Sparkler form

A Glitter or Sparkler Visitation is quick and fleeting. It's usually a random out of the corner of your eye visit and can precede you seeing a full vision visitation. Some people only experience this level.

IF you fleetingly see this form of visitation you are always able to call them up and see this form. If you **do** have this ability, there is a high probability of being able to see them on demand and for a sustained period of time. You go!

3. Vision

This is the translucent "ghost" level look. Spirit will take on the form that you knew and are familiar with. This Spirit visitation requires the most amount of electromagnetic manipulation on their part.

4. Orbs

Orbs are a distinctly different form of an energy presence visit.

An Orb is a circular ball of electromagnetic mass that is a singular energy entity and energy form classification unto itself. (YouTube video 49) Spirits often use Orb forms to visit. Orbs are usually seen at twilight and later. White orbs are positive energy and respond to love and happy places and occasions. They even emit their own electronic sounds which can be recorder and show up quite often in photographs, on night vision surveillance cameras and videos.

Orbs can also denote a Spirit's visit to their special place. Selena the cat's Orb visited her Garden spot on multiple occasions after transition.

When Jessie the Cockatiel was alive, she liked to sit on Dwayne's shoulder; it was one of her special places.

After she transitioned she continued to do so in Orb form. Orbs are a way Spirit lets you know they are still hanging out with you. You can always ask who they are to identify them as taught in a previous section.

Seeing Spirits

Many individuals are so rattled by a vision visitation that they think it's not controllable. It is! (YouTube video 71)

You are in control of your earth space.
You can always command a Spirit to leave. (YouTube video 139).
Or ask them to extend their Visitation either specifically or as they so choose. When I do a reading, I ask Spirit to stay until all questions are answered. In over 20 years I've only had 2 cats walk out early.

IF you ever get a random or questionable visitation from any Spirit that you don't know or didn't summon, be sure to ask these questions
* Are you here for my Highest and best Good?
* Who are you?
* Who do you work for?
* Why are you here?
* What do you want me to know?
* Show me what you want me to know now.

They will answer you telepathically or you'll have a translatable feeling in your heart.

Lessons from Loved Ones in Heaven
How to Connect with your Loved One on the Other Side
to Heal from Loss

How to See a Spirit

If you have seen glimpses, it's possible you will be able to sustain the energy connection to see Spirits.

When you look at a Spirit, as I have mentioned before, it will appear like a "see through" steam, cloudy or sparkly, flashy luminous iridescent version of what they looked like on earth. Usually Spirit will present themselves in a healthy mid-life physical form. People Spirits oftentimes will wear your or their favorite clothes to help you recognize them!

Step 1: Ask your deceased person or pet energy to show up.
I ask and it is my intent to contact the energy previously known as _____,
so that I can feel him here NOW.

Step 2: Once your departed person or pet has responded, identify and locate their energy presence. Then state the following.

Prayer to See Spirit

I ask and it is my intent to see <u>deceased name</u> Spirit form now, I ask and it is my intent to see my deceased __ name ___Spirit form now, I ask and it is my intent to see my deceased __name__) Spirit form now.

2. Then close your eyes tight and say, "shift energy and refocus now."

3. Open your eyes softly, try not to blink. Call them by their earth name and say
_____ show yourself to me, in front of me NOW, show yourself to me, in front of me now, show yourself to me, in front of me now.

If you have this skill set, in time they will show up!!! Be patient. If you have glanced them out of the corner of your eye, now specifically ask them to "show up **in front of** me," so you will have a very clear image of them!

Not getting an immediate response is most likely your body not being sensitized and accustomed to seeing and holding that type of energy connection. Learning to see energy can be activated immediately or gradually. Practice.

When I ask to see Spirit, it takes about 3 to 5 seconds. For over two decades, I always close my eyes after initiating my request and then reopen them to see Spirit.

ORBS can be called in with the same prayer. Just change the word Spirit form to Orb form. There are some apps that teach you to film Orbs. Use at your own risk and say your Protection prayer before beginning!

If you are open to randomly seeing a **specific** (key) Spirit, give them permission to visit when they so choose. They WILL visit! Do not provide an open invitation to any and all Spirits. **Be very specific.**

I often see Possum Kitty running from room to room and Hairy Kitty's Spirit sleeping in my open office drawer. Sometimes I see my yellow lab "Boo Bear" running across the golf course with his ball showing me he's happy.

And then there's Mike sneaking in. I usually see him standing on the other side of the room supporting whatever I'm doing at the moment. He knows his Spirit **still** rattles my soul, but he'll gently smile and the forever in his eyes melts my heart. I just say thank you Mikey and go have a good short commemorative cry!

Some individuals have indicated they are afraid of doing this exercise because it may be harmful or bring in unwanted energies or entities. When you say the Protection prayer that is written earlier in this book, you are fully and completely covered.

I use that Prayer every day. IF you draw in negative energies and entities because **you changed some words** or **forgot the Protection prayer,** watch my YouTube Video 139 and clean up your space immediately.

Some people have asked about using Ouija boards and other methods to bring in Spirit. Not a good idea!!
NEVER, NEVER, EVER!

Fun facts: The hour that most unrequested Spirits visit earth is 4 am and its usually a male presence. Guardian Angels do most of their work in Dreams.

Do you want more information during Spirit visits?
When Spirit makes time to get your attention, whether through a whisper in your mind's ear or a warm nudge in your heart, or the fact that they have taken the time to reformulate for you to see them, it's an opportune time to ask for more information. They obviously have something they want to relate to you.

Request for More Information

Say: "<u>Spirit's name</u> show me what I need to know about you now."
Or "tell me what you want me to know now"
So be it, it is done, Thank you.

You can also say this request while they are making any connection, appearance or communication effort. I use both of these questions in my readings to get different information.

Remember, repeating each phrase 3 times makes it REAL clear! Then listen to what you hear in your heart. Be sure to thank them for showing up. Also, be sure to invite them to return anytime they choose if you want them to do so!

It will take a while for you to get used to accessing another frequency. Practice makes perfect!!! Try to practice when you can focus and not be distracted.

Being able to do this will change your life and open your awareness and understanding. If you "can't" do this particular technique don't be upset.

Not all people can **see** Spirits, however,
Everyone can connect and communicate!

Lessons from Loved Ones in Heaven
How to Connect with your Loved One on the Other Side
to Heal from Loss

Communication with Spirit

Everyone can talk to **their** Spirit person or pet because they are intimately connected at the heart level.
Not everyone can talk to **all** Spirits.
See the difference?

That's why when advertising psychic or animal communication classes, usually the script says, "everyone can talk to loved ones or their animals." They just leave off the specific words of their **own** person or animal.

Many grieving pet parents flock to those advertisements, take several discounted courses or CD classes and become certified as an animal communicator by someone who hasn't even practiced as a professional.

Warning- before you take any class to get certified by someone for mediumship, as a psychic or animal communicator, check to see how long the teacher has **earned a living** at their profession. YouTube video 237

A great teacher should have a long-standing income producing, trustworthy experience record to be able to impart anything worthwhile to you. A person who makes a living with their skills must be real in order to sustain their business and reputation. Longevity using their Gift as their sole profession is the key.

You don't want to pay for, attend and then discover you can't talk to other people or animals on an ongoing basis. That's the downside of a lot of advertising. You think you can communicate after being "certified" for a hypothetical $49.00 from a CD, training webinar, seminar, interactive study weekend or home study class and in the real world, it just doesn't work.

What you're going to learn in my book is how to have a conversation with **your** Spirit.

Spirit communication is hearing in your heart, receiving telepathic thoughts from your "mine only" Spirit (YouTube Video 70), intuitively experiencing translatable feelings or just talking face to face with them like I do.

Talking to **all** Spirits is my Gift. I can access a multitude of energy frequencies in past, present and future realms to get any information.

Clients ask, since you talk to animals, can you talk to people Spirits? Yes.
I love to talk with animal spirits and prefer to keep my human communication limited and special with

only my Mikey. On rare occasions, I help friends talk to their people Spirits when they have a deep, urgent and important need to connect.

All **you** need to do is access the energy connection you had in your earth life together to activate a conversation with your person or pet. Then erase any doubt that you can't do it! Losing doubt is a process of gaining more and more faith in the **ongoing** relationship you now share in this new journey.

Why would you want to communicate with Spirit?

Because you might have a lot of unanswered questions, need advice, are curious about their new life or are just lonesome for them. They are available 24/ 7/ 365. NO waiting required. If someone tells you, you have to wait for a while, they are **wrong**! I watch and talk to Spirits while they are going through the transition process, crossing over the death line and emerging into all there is as a new Spirit form.

Talk out loud and encourage them to help you create a better connection to communicate! Accepting, praising and interacting with your Spirit partner motivates more communication with the Other Side! Remember you were a team on Earth, now you are a team on Earth and the Other Side.

Lessons from Loved Ones in Heaven
How to Connect with your Loved One on the Other Side
to Heal from Loss

Start the Conversation

It's **never** too late to start the conversation. No matter how long they have been gone, it's never too late to talk to Spirit.

First and foremost, talk to your Spirit as if they are with you, they are! Out loud or from your head or heart, either way works. They're waiting to begin.

If you want to chat out loud in public, go ahead and do so. In today's world people will think you're wearing a cell phone ear bud or microphone and talking on the phone!

The more discussion you have with Spirit the more they will interface with you! They sound like a different slightly altered voice than yours. Some Spirits have very distinct tones. Others almost seem too familiar like you're talking to yourself. If you get an immediate answer you are not! Praise them, they'll do more of it.

Once you start talking you'll feel less of a void. Mike and I have ongoing conversations, so much so that at times, I have to tell him to leave me alone.

It's not unusual behavior to tell a Spirit when you are ready to chat. Immediately after his death, there was no way I could ever fathom the thought of sending Mike away. He's still the chatty persona in Spirit that he was on earth, so every now and then I need some me time.

YouTube Video 10 illustrates a time when you think that you start crying for no reason when in fact it's your favorite Spirit moving in closer to tug at your heart strings and begin a conversation.

Be grateful that they are assertive no matter what your earth receptivity is at that moment. Don't discourage them early on. Say thanks for being here. Then when your emotions smooth out you can say, I'm ready to talk now.

How to Talk with a Specific Spirit

To me, a reading or communication session with Spirit is sacred. Initially, that was the only way I could connect with Mike before my Gift was activated. I feel a great responsibility, accountability and honor to provide the most profound, candid and detailed information I can while helping my clients. As you begin, I suggest you take your communication seriously until you are confident enough to be playful. It's the most life changing and deepest conversations of your hearts and souls.

This is not a long-distance communication as differentiated in some training classes. It's your personal energy communicating with a specific Spirit energy through the bond you already have. Just that simple.

You might want to alert Spirit beforehand when or why you want to talk with them.
Just say out loud or in your heart that you want to chat tomorrow night or can we talk about whenever. This will provide a heads up in their endless time surroundings, so they'll be looking for your call.

Contrary to what is taught, you do not have to meditate, do any breathing exercises or perform any special rituals or visualize anything before you begin nor set up a sacred space. However, if you feel a routine is necessary or it resonates with you, then please start the process your way.

All you need to do is get quiet in your mind and relax using whatever technique that works for you. I close my eyes for a few seconds and take a deep breath before each reading. That's it!

Sometimes taking a shower or bath beforehand will clear your energy field and have you in a calm smooth place. After a long walk unwinding from the day's busyness is also a good time. So is just before going to sleep or right after waking up before the day's activities get going.

Here's the deal, all you need to do is be calm, and focused on being receptive to listening to whatever Spirit wants to say. Know your heart's love will connect and protect you. It's not like your soul has never whispered to them before. The **only** difference now is that you want to receive a response in a definite timeframe.

Situate and settle yourself in a place without interference where you can devote total focus to the discussion you are about to begin. Usually I take my shoes off because it's more grounding for me, but not a necessity.

I suggest you also have a favorite photograph of your person or pet clearly showing their eyes. I believe more photos allow better access to the energy when you are beginning. Don't stare at the picture(s) until after the beginning prayer when you are ready to start communication. Later when you become accustomed to their energetic interchange, you can talk anywhere, anytime without any props.

The fact that you now know and recognize what your pet or person's presence feels like, is an added bonus. Their communication will emanate from that same energy source and feel the same.

The best part of communicating with your Spirit is that you never know what they will say. The worst part is that you never know what they will share now that there are no repercussions. Oftentimes, there is **no order** as they present random information. I have found that coming in with a list of questions stifles and limits responses. Save those specific questions until the end.

Be open to whatever and however Spirit wants to share whether you want to hear it or not. That way you'll receive more interesting and OMG content.

I suggest that you keep a pen and pad handy, so you won't get overwhelmed and forget what they say.

Ask each Spirit's permission to speak with them. In 20 years of sessions, only 3 Spirits have declined. Why would they decline? Could be timing or just plain "I don't want to talk to anyone" as one Bischon stated. It's also possible that your emotions are in the way or your intention for a 2-way open and candid conversation is not pure. I always believe my clients are brought to me by the Spirits who know their person needs to have in-depth, extremely personal, specific and detailed answers and life purpose directives without any expectations or filters.

It is a requirement that you have no expectations!

Having no expectations or filters when you listen to what Spirit says is **the hardest** thing to do. Being neutral and remaining open will reap the greatest, purest and most profound testimonies.

If you are unsuccessful today, don't get worked up. This does **not** mean Spirit is not going to participate. Be patient and try again later or on another day.

Factually, Spirit may take a while to get everyone on the same time frame. Mike always loved to talk to me in the shower or while I'm on the toilet because he had a sequestered audience. We stopped that practice early on!

Ask or talk about whatever you want to know. Even ask what **Spirit** wants you to know. It's my belief that if you go into the conversation with a set of limiting questions, you get limited responses. I leave all parameters wide open. Nothing is off limits.

Most people will receive thoughts, feelings, impressions and images which is called telepathic communication. Some of you may have Spirit show up as a steam form vision in front of you like I do, and be ready for a talk. Don't be afraid, how comforting and wonderful!

Spirit always delivers messages **from their point of view** and verbiage. Because you call something one thing, does **not** mean your person or pet will call it the exact same thing. You may have to ask yourself, how do I connect with this concept. Oftentimes with people and pets you may have to decipher the delivery or ask them to be clearer. In time, you'll develop a natural rhythmic exchange.

Some individuals may feel disappointed with the simplicity of the following instructions to communicate with your Loved One. All the training classes, workshops and weekend retreats boil it down to the same things.

Lessons from Loved Ones in Heaven
How to Connect with your Loved One on the Other Side
to Heal from Loss

1. Place yourself in a calm and non-disruptive environment

2. Open your mind and heart to the possibility of this actually working

3. Protect yourself

4. Ask permission

5. Ask the specific Spirit to be present for your conversation

6. Know how to identify and validate the energy you want to connect with

7. Begin looking at the photos you have

8. Then ask or chat away with **no** expectations, filters or limiting parameters!

9. Close the session and disconnect from your Spirit after your conversation.

10. Then you can add come and visit or chat whenever. It's your choice.

11. Thank Spirit for participating.

You already have an established relationship and bond. Now you want to connect and communicate with them on the Other Side. There is no special magic, intent or focus more powerful than direct heart to soul love based conversations with a **specific** Spirit.

Just do it!

Say Protection Prayer

Ask permission to talk with a specific Spirit.

Ask that specific Spirit's energy to come be in your presence. Validate this with the open hand feeling energy technique.

Say Communication prayer

Thank you for the Gift of healing energy. Surround me, shield me, fill me, ground and protect me with the Christ White Light.
(Use whatever your Higher Power is called)

I ask all those in charge of my Soul's contract, all those in charge of <u>Spirit's name</u> soul's contract to come and work with us now.

I ask all my angels and all <u>Spirit's name</u> angels to come and share information with me now only for our highest and best good.

I ask that I have no expectations of this communication so the energy will be pure and the information not be tainted.

I ask that I have no human filters for this communication so the information will be pure and the energy will not be tainted.

Use me. Use me. Use me for our conversations highest and best good.
So be it, it is done. Thank you.

Both the Protection and Communication prayer will ensure that you are talking **only** to your special Spirit. I use both for every Reading.

Spread your pictures out like a collage in front of you. I prefer to use a lot of pictures that exhibit different moods and attitudes. This provides Spirit multiple ways to initiate a conversation. You'll get better and more input when you do this.

Look at each photo to determine which one "pulls" or immediately gets your attention. Look at that outstanding photo and ask "Spirit what do you want to tell me." Then listen and move to the next photo.

When I look at a photo I immediately start getting information. I share with my client who then verifies that I have the correct Spirit to chat with. Spirit walks in so I can see them while sharing those details. We begin the Reading.

I always begin by asking **simple** straightforward questions like "is there anything you want me to know?" Prepare other questions in advance so you have your emotions in check before your chat. Remember not everything has to be answered on the first conversation.

If you're uncomfortable and having trouble getting answers, ask Spirit to ask **you** questions. That **always** starts a conversation!

As Spirit answers, you will begin to pick up mental observations. Carry on your conversation based upon the impressions you received. You can also ask Spirit to help you decipher what they say such as "tell me more about what you mean," "Please clarify that for me." They will.

People Spirits usually relay discussion descriptions in verbiage and concepts that you can understand and in the language, you each know. You will hear them in a recognizable manner. Pet Spirits share from their perspective in a language you can understand.

When you feel the session is coming to an end, ask "is that all for today?" I've had several Spirits say "I'm through now". Or you could say "may I ask a few more questions". Spirit will let you know if it's OK.

Don't be so needy to communicate that you get pushy or tired. You have forever to continue talking! When you are tired you **will not** get clear information.

You can also ask "when is a good time to talk", or "when would Spirit suggest that you talk again." Spirit is never short on opinions.

How to Close a Session

To close your energetic Earth to Other Side connection for this conversation, say:
Thank you for sharing with me or us (whoever on earth is attending the session). I now remove, release and detach from <u>Spirit's Name's</u> energy, so be it, it is done.

The release prayer closes the "opening" with the Other Side. It's another form of protection so you don't get unexpected visitors. Spirit is then free to come and go without directly affecting your energy field. The release does not mean forever, it just means for that conversation. Spirit remains just as near and interactive with you as before.

Communication with your Spirit is not magical or hard to do when it's a heart to heart, energy to energy established personal relationship.

Crying during your communication is perfectly all right. Spirit comments can be so profound, unbridled, raw, sensitive and on point that tears are normal. However, don't allow crying to be so disruptive that it breaks your concentration and pushes away the energetic connection.

*****

The KEY to any and all Spirit Connection or Communication is to ASK.

Ask to be shown or told in a way you can easily understand the reason of why you didn't get a Sign, Dream, Communication response or whatever.

Ask yourself what are you doing to disrupt the energy.

Ask why this <u>fill in the blank</u> isn't working.

Ask, ask, ask.

In perfect timing you will **always** get the answer for your Highest and best good!

What I've learned

This bears repeating. Before you dismiss any answers or data, write the descriptions down and think about it later. In time, you'll figure it out. Over time you'll develop a dialogue exchange that you can easily understand. Pets more often than people use **their own interpretation and perception** of what something is in their communication.

Ex: The cat said, "I love the red round rolly thing." The parent denied knowing anything about that. One month later, she was cleaning under her bed and found a red PVC pipe that the cat liked to climb inside and roll around in on the floor, thus the "red round rolly thing."

Communication mistakes

Thinking this exchange is scary, evil or anything else that's not an exchange of the pure love you shared.

Being too tired

Being pushy or demanding with Spirit

Pre- deciding (choosing to think) that you can't connect.

Allowing outside activity to distract your focus.

Being sick, in a bad mood or having major attitude. Your mind needs to be clean and clear.

Emotional filters; crying, anger, extreme guilt, blame, fear, etc.

Expectations about what and how you want Spirit to react and say to you.

Limiting and telling Spirit what to talk about.

Not allowing Spirit to communicate when they want to share

Rushing the conversation.

Jumping to conclusions- ask Spirit to verify what you assumed they meant.

Discouraging sensitive feelings or needs subjects.

Avoiding or dismissing Spirit advice.

Being judgmental of Spirit opinions.

Allowing your discomfort to color Spirit responses.

Being closeminded to anything- new insights, perceptions and suggestions.

Blowing off that a Spirit could teach you anything

Dismissing Truth because you don't want to hear it.

Now that you can access your Loved Ones, let's renovate the rest of your new life. You can always ask Spirit's opinions, guidance and approval to see how you're doing.

Lessons from Loved Ones in Heaven
How to Connect with your Loved One on the Other Side
to Heal from Loss

Chapter 5- Rebuilding Your Life

Identify your Feelings

No matter how Spiritual, your human life and feelings need to be addressed and rejuvenated too. Loss wreaks havoc with every part of your being.

Shock & Numbness

When Shock is overwhelming you, take a time out. When all the details are too much, give yourself a break!

Numbness helps balance your shock. It calms things down to feeling nothing! When you're too numb to concentrate or even be present, you won't feel good. Nothing is interesting and everything is "too much to handle," sometimes even getting out of bed.

If you're floundering by being overwhelmed, it's essential to mentally and emotionally process all that you have been dealt. Do not be ashamed to feel overwhelmed with all the details and turmoil. It's natural!

The key is **to limit the time you allow yourself to be overwhelmed.** Set aside a few hours or no more than 3 days to get quiet and regroup mentally. Shut out all "well-wishers" and even family or pets if necessary during this time to regroup.

Lessons from Loved Ones in Heaven
How to Connect with your Loved One on the Other Side
to Heal from Loss

Every person that has been touched by your loss needs time alone to "grasp" the situation, gain more understanding, gather their strength and reflect on the decisions to be made going forward.

When you just can't handle
ONE >>>>MORE>>>THING!
And you don't have the stamina for
ONE>>>MORE>>>THING>>>>>>>>>
cry, rest, yell, vent, read, whatever it takes, then sleep. Going forward comes **after** your "time out" for a sanity break.

Remember, Sleep is healing!!! And so is a good cry, don't be ashamed to do so!

Hurt

Crying is usually the first manifestation of feeling hurt after shock and numbness fades. It's PERFECTLY OK!
It's normal and energetically cleansing. Crying clears out grieving energy which makes way for the new positive healing energy.

Release the pain, the fear, the frustration, whatever needs to go. Cry it out! Then take a nap. You'll wake refreshed and motivated to go forward or cry some more!

Did you know that Crying is also the No 1 Sign that your loved one in Spirit is close and near? Please watch my YouTube videos 10 & 147.

There is nothing wrong with positive crying. It's healthy and helpful. Having a little cry can honor your love connection many years afterwards. I still shed a few tears for Mike almost 21 years later. Afterwards I smile and say thank you for being a part of my journey and in my life!

Lessons from Loved Ones in Heaven
How to Connect with your Loved One on the Other Side
to Heal from Loss

Anniversaries and Special Occasions

The first Anniversary is tough because it marks that ONE YEAR has passed and you're still sensitive to and acutely aware of your earth loss. Although growing older is inevitable, how you process Anniversaries is a choice.

Why do these events trigger your heart? Inherently it's supposed to be a celebration but you don't feel like celebrating. It's a reminder that it's the worst day of your life contrasted to the good days of your life before that time. The lack of" what was" is the dividing line.

You don't get over loving just because the person or pet is not there. You remember how their love and your joy felt years ago. Not having the physical earth suit to cuddle anymore is what creates a flat line in your heart and mind. It feels painful when you can't interact physically like you used to do.

Anniversaries trigger good and bad feelings in an inseparable basket of emotions. On regular days, you think about your beloved as how they were and might have been. The yearly marker tends to bring up future hopes, and dreams you planned or wanted to share together. And when that happens, you're slammed in the heart with the fact that you have to move alone. (Hint- not really!)

Lessons from Loved Ones in Heaven
How to Connect with your Loved One on the Other Side
to Heal from Loss

Anniversaries, birthdays and special occasions aren't separated in your mind because it's all jumbled up in the great pain of loss and you're supposed to be celebrating activities of joy. Pick joy! Say no to the pain and yes to the joy! How do you do that?

Compartmentalize the pain. That's the essential ingredient. Limit the time you scroll through the painful activities, lessons or itemize the bad. Maximize the review of "happies." That way the pain will become less frequent.

At year 17 I forgot Mike's Birthday. I figured I should and would feel horrible and guilty. I didn't. It was a monumental marker indicating that I was enjoying his Spirit so much in my daily routine, that he had to remind me I forgot!

So, I threw a birthday party that night. I bought cards, cooked his favorite food and even did a cake. When it came time to blow out the candles they were just flickering away. I knew it was Mike letting me know that he was with me and appreciating my efforts. He even messed with the music, so I would know which song was ours.

It is Ok to also have pity parties on occasion. The key is to only allow yourself a limited time to "go there." After the initial Loss scenario, only your very best supporters and friends will continue an ongoing pity party. Spirit of course, is kindly waiting for you to finish that human grief phase so you can get on with the business of living together in a different way.

There will come a time when **no one else** but you will want to be around your pity party. Why? Because it's a downer and may trigger their hurtful emotions.

It boils down to this. Anniversaries, birthdays and special occasions are like a chunk of gourmet cheese that has been sitting out since the loss occurred. You enjoy the good cheese and don't feel good if you eat the molded part.

You have a **choice,** shave off the mold and savor the essence of the richer aged cheese or not. I hope you choose to savor their life and not let your loss grow mold in your mind.

It's not the letting go that hurts in the long run, it's the holding onto "what was" and disregarding all that you have to share from now on!

Lessons from Loved Ones in Heaven
How to Connect with your Loved One on the Other Side
to Heal from Loss

Loneliness

I manically held onto and replayed Mike's answering machine message over and over and memorized prerecorded occasion cards. Listening to his voice I cried, pleaded, yelled, wailed, screamed, and hoped it would make everything Ok. Simply said: YOU are the one who has to handle your loss!

Are you aware that you are never alone? Never Ever! Now that you know how, talk with your Spirit, ask for Signs and y'all get busy with your new life.

Did you know that you also have Universal Helpers- Angels, Guides and Guardians that are specifically assigned to your life while you are on Earth? God (or your Higher Power) and your Universal Guardians, Angels, Guides and Helpers are in charge of your Soul's contract. That's why They watch over you and are ready to assist you at ANY time for anything. If you don't call on your Universal assistants, or ask Their help, they just sit around the Universe very bored. Use the communication techniques to ask questions and get their help!

In addition to your special Spirit, your Heavenly helpers are also **full** of answers, assistance and gifts you never request. Don't waste a fabulous resource and the "Higher Power" available to explicitly help you by omission. Think about what you might be missing by NOT praying or asking for assistance when you feel alone. I talk with Mike **and** my Heavenly guidance.

To me, nighttime loneliness is the worst! Even with Mike's energy there, I still miss being able to hug and hold his "suit." That is a normal human response.

And when I get caught up in the Human aspect and set aside my spiritual awareness, nights can be haunting, hurting and long no matter who I know is watching over me.

That's when I ask my Angels to protect me and keep me safe from any and all harm. Oftentimes, I invite Mike or my pets to come spend the night. You can have great uninterrupted conversations for clarity, closure, advice and just plain ole gossip. Its like a Spiritual sleep over.
Talk to them!!! It takes the edge off.

Isolation

An isolated environment deadens your thinking and will to live.

Retreating into isolation or under the sheets gets you nowhere, and breeds inactivity and depression. Being a spectator and not a participator will lead to a fragile "I can't do this," or "I need help" emotional response that can take away your independence. It's the old "use it or lose it" adage. Try to interact with others even if you are initially faking it!

I tried sequestering myself for 3 years, I just got older and became nervous and depressed when being around people. My once toney and active self, had turned into an out of shape couch potato, muffin top, saddle bagged, out of breath person with bad hair that I did not recognize nor even care about.

This is not a time to save activities for "later." Break out of your old routines and create variety by exploring everything you ever wanted to try. You're not going haywire, it's merely a diversion for your mind to take a rest and to look at the life around you. Hopefully to inspire you to re-engage in life again.

Try looking at cookbooks; it will lead you to a recipe that may find its way to your plate. Reading about Paris, not only expands your awareness, it may reignite your travel dreams by inspiring places you want to go. These or any expansive activity builds dreams for future probability. The Bucket List movie addresses the pluses of making a dream list and then doing it! This exercise revs up all your systems and is especially helpful when you feel there is no future.

Create Activities

Activity stimulates your mind to LIVE! When you grow old and unable to move around, you'll have wonderful stories to tell and times to celebrate. If you can't go alone, have someone take you for a drive, to a new restaurant, or to the movies etc. When you can't face going out, bring the people to you, that counts as interaction. This helps divert your mind from thinking about what was!

Being active (even walking or other physical exercises raises your endorphins to elevate your mood) keeps your energy moving and contributes to creating a psyche that wants to survive even though now, you feel like you're just barely getting by.

The more you do, the better you will adjust to being able to do more. Plan activities for a week or months down the road to have a future! **You must choose to have an interactive future!**

My great grandmother always said, "make memories, so when you can't do anything but sit, you'll have lots to recall and talk about."

Express Your Feelings

Another way to combat missing their earth suit is to vent feelings out loud and with others. Anyone who hasn't been in a similar position **won't** understand. It's hard to relate to people who have never suffered a loss and insist on giving you chirpy advice and cheerleader support. (At least they're being positive.)

Talk truthfully about your feelings. Vent till it's all out! It's therapeutic to express concerns and to release frustration.
However, limit the time you let off steam (key) and then move on.

You can write letters to your beloved to release all you want to say. You can create Scrapbooks to celebrate your journey and purge those feelings as you put it together.

I made sit down dinners for Mike and we discussed everything I wanted to address. I didn't eat much but it made me feel connected. We celebrated birthdays, anniversaries and all of our special events and I told him everything. Although I felt good after our intimate meetings, I needed more. Next, I tried Support groups.

Support Groups

Support groups come in all flavors and sizes, in person, in healthcare facilities, churches and other organizations and online. They are intended to provide substantive and positive emotional, mental and sometimes spiritual support. Expressing feelings about your loss is healthy in the right environment.

If you can't physically get to a support group or use the Internet, create a phone group of people who have had similar experiences. You'll feel less forgotten, deserted and socially isolated with phone pals. The human bond is about sharing with someone who understands!

*** You're invited to share your feelings, concerns and questions in our global Facebook Grief Recovery group focusing on people called Lessons from Loved ones in Heaven in Loving Memory.

*** You're also invited to join my global Pet loss group on Facebook about Animal Life After Death. Frankie Johnson is our professional bereavement counselor.

The Positive Support Group

A proactive support group is one that promotes learning, positive growth and helps facilitate personal improvement and empowerment while expanding your horizons. They're a blessing in your life.

A positive group leader is open minded and inspired to become more educated. They are not intimidated by unanswerable questions This leader encourages you to ask questions that require more research to challenge each member to think beyond their present circumstances. This group meets you where you are when you enter, and offer uplifting support. Rather than continuously "poor babying" you, they provide mind expanding learning opportunities and advice.

They encourage members to extend their thinking and provide techniques and tools to promote individual achievement like receiving Signs, by sharing interactive personal perspectives from group member experiences and allow everyone to be an inspiration to someone else. **It's a "can do" group!**

This group believes in Transition and celebrates that Spirits are alive, well and continuing their Love with you in a different way.

The Negative Support Group
From your introduction "story" to your sad weekly tale of woe, this group meets only to **rehash** and illuminate your personal devastation and embrace the "dead end and gone" attitude.

This is a "victim of loss" group commiserating and connecting through negative experience sharing at the highest level of disguise. Initially you think how wonderful that they understand how you feel, and are so compassionate and empathetic.

No matter how much you think that this group is helping you, they are NOT! They want to talk about your misery, and not expand your awareness nor ask you to think outside of the loss of death.

You will find endless talking about and sharing bad experiences that reinforce a "stuck" atmosphere in this group LEAVE. It's bonding by perpetual "doom gloom downers." In this group, you receive more recognition and attention for being the victim of your plight. By associating with these people you're contributing to your mental and emotional destruction.

It should be of great concern to be in a group that does nothing but recount what was and is unhappily going on in the life of its participants. Over and over! Inevitably this negatively impacts your mind and pulls your emotions down even further. What would your Beloved Spirit have to say about this group????

Ever noticed the mood in a room after you've recounted all the horrible things that have occurred? You've already lived your "sad story" so why keep reactivating it? As long as you are stuck in what "was," you're living in the past and no one goes away refreshed, revived and full of hope.

Many folks after years, are **still** telling the same story that "I can't get over it" (**that's their choice**) with every embellished detail just to keep the conversation vibrant with the drama they endured. Actually, healing and recovering, my goodness, then they would need to create a fulfilling life and do something <u>other than</u> talk about themselves and the problems created by their loss.

I know a woman who after fifteen years of therapy and ten years in every support group or chat room she could find, started her own support group because no one wanted to hear her repetitive victim stories anymore.

Research substantiates that recounting your horror story and reading the countless negative venting of others **does NOT** promote healthy responses.

By allowing yourself to be and marking yourself as a victim, YOU are the only one who will lose the respect and patience of those who encourage and support your healing.

You are also dishonoring the life spent with your Loved One. They want you to be happy and continuing your connection with them in Joy. They want to help you have a better life not one of doom gloom sadness.

Muster the courage to break from your neediness to rely on the loss to give your life meaning. If you keep wallowing in your unhappy existence, you can rest assured that less and less people and friends will stay around.

Rather than a commiseration Band-aid, you can learn to tell a story that shares your "learning opportunity" to help others. Teach them about Transition, connecting and communicating with Spirit and celebrating all things positive.

Acceptance is one thing, denial or head in the sand attitude is another. Allowing yourself to be a victim drains you. Having a problem and addressing it with the "pity poor me" approach is futile. It may elicit help for a while, but the key here is "for a while." Choose to give up the pity party and poor baby designation. Instead, use your time learning how to restore and regenerate your life and to connect and communicate with your favorite Spirit.

So, analyze the dynamics of the group you are in to determine if you are evolving or rehashing. If your group doesn't embrace open mindedness, shuts down a greater awareness and learning experiences in all areas of your life, I hope you choose to leave!

Since, no one in a negative group cares whether you move forward or not, **unless you choose to grow**, you will remain in the same mental condition that brought you into the group in the first place.

I call that emotional state "Whatever-land!"

"Whatever- land"

My Loved one is dead. I'm not learning about that spiritual stuff. This is my belief and what I was taught. I'm not changing my mind. My Loved one is dead and the rest of my life is over.

When you are so closeminded about YOUR loss, you are completely discounting the good your beloved contributed. It's all about you.

Denial is a fatal fantasy. Anytime you run away from something or have your head in the sand so to speak, you can and most likely will be miserable. Not "doing anything" out of fear is a "safety net" that enables poor choices with you as the victim. Your choice to be broken, causes you to miss a lot of joyous experiences and wonderful daily expressions of love.

ONLY YOU can break through **your** excuses, justifications and smoke screens. Until you get REAL with yourself, face, **identify** and **remove** negative and self-limiting barriers, you'll never truly go forward in any area of your life or be happy.

The "whatever" attitude is the mindset to
NOT deal with anything that you need to deal with.

A "whatever" attitude denotes an early stage of depression. I lived in this state for several years. It's like your life is on the same gerbil wheel going around and round yet getting nowhere. It's the place you go when you choose not to handle life. "Whatever, who cares."

Do you make these or similar statements?
- "Whatever"
- "I feel empty inside, nothing interests me anymore."
- "I'm not excited about anything."
- "I'm just existing."
- "I'm getting by the best way I know how."
- "I just don't care anymore."
- "Why bother?"
- "Who cares?"
- "What's the use, I don't feel anything."
- "I just don't have any get up and go
- "I tried for a while, but "
- "I don't want to even be involved or love again."
- "Just leave me alone!"

A serious, mean it to your core "leave me alone" is the time for medical intervention for depression. A "leave me alone for a while" is honoring your space to regroup, or just be.

The "whatever" state of mind is hard to combat because there is validity in some of the things you are saying. It's also a barometer of how you are handling your obstacles and a red flag to those around you that you need some help in lifting yourself up. This is usually the time to join a positive support group as outlined in an earlier chapter. It's obvious that you need some shoring up!

Hoisting yourself up is a hard thing to do. It took me over 7 years to emotionally recover from Mike's sudden death. I'm not just blowing smoke about how to get out of this, I had to learn to survive me.

When you live in a "whatever" state, your life choices are NOT working for you. Resolving the "whatever" attitude is the key to moving forward. Take a step, a baby step, a side step, any movement to leave the "whatever" space. The goal is to put the twinkle back in your eye and reignite your desire to live, hope and dream again.

Check point:
Look at yourself in the mirror to see if you have any of these signs:
• Do you have flat, dead looking, nobody is home eyes staring back at you?

• Are you round shouldered, worn out looking, disheveled, tired with poor hygiene and blah-faced with no emotions?

• When looking at yourself. do you say, "I don't know who that person is and I really don't care?"

If yes is your answer, you need to find and reclaim yourself out of "whatever" land!
It takes your inner core looking at "who IS that in the mirror, it's not me" recognition to ignite your Soul.

There will come a day, when deep inside you've had all the heartache, nothingness, "whatever" you can handle. Just by your decision that
"something HAS to change! I can't live like this anymore!"
Now, your "down" starts UP!

How to Get Out of "Whatever" Land

Even while talking with Spirit and getting Signs, you still probably feel like you're muddling through the remnants of your life. It takes time to cultivate a new individual emotional strength.

Emotional stamina and an ongoing relationship with Spirit will fortify your staying power throughout this healing journey. If you can't manage this program on your own, please get a friend to encourage and work with you through these steps and or seek professional help.

This is NOT a time to avoid solutions. Begin by setting a specific calendar date to start getting YOU back! Don't sequester yourself with Spirit and not interact with other human beings.

Step 1 is the hardest part- actually getting going! Do anything that makes you feel "kinda good." Examples: Watch the movie that you've seen 100 times that STILL makes you laugh, gardening outside or petting your other fur babies. If allowed have a food treat. Go for it! Wash or comb your hair, shave, spruce up your personal hygiene. Get a massage. This is your first mini step- one day at a time. Ask Spirit what to do, they know you best.

Step 2 add more "kinda good" soul-satisfying things at least every other day. Build up to once a day!
Make yourself do this, NO excuses.
As Nike ads say: "Just Do it!"
Examples:
Call someone just to chat. You don't even have to pay attention to what they are saying. It's the human connection that matters.
Start some form of physical movement, anything different from your usual isolated rut.

Go outside (there is a sky), buy and smell fresh flowers for your table, listen to a new music download or get another pet. The "new this and that" activates you remembering good things.

Spirit is never upset when you add love into your life. **Spirit will not feel replaced nor dishonored**. They know how much love you have to give and want you to use it! When your heart is ready, move forward! Sometimes it's the companionship that helps you heal.

Step 3 Now that you're progressing a little at a time. (Wahoo!) Make a list or collect pictures or coupons about things that would make you feel good.
Create a "happy" today not 3 years from now. Clip a restaurant or movie coupon and go tomorrow night.

Each tiny "do-it-this-day" activity stretches your participation in life and bolsters hope. You may be surprised by enjoying yourself.

Soon you'll progress to weekly then monthly "nudgies" that create variety and move you out of your doldrums, engage you with living people and get you thinking about "future plans."

Examples: Have a friend ride you around in their car. Make yourself spend an allotted time (like an hour) away from your safe comfort zone. Start something to enhance your personal appearance: (new robe, haircut, lipstick, manicure, great smelling moisture cream or wipe, exercise activity, IPOD, PDA, computer games, etc.)

Gradually add to your "I'm worth it" time. Increase the number of different activities and people involved. Friends count!!! Stop moping around.

Step 4 When you feel comfortable, step over the wall you've created to survive. Start moving about in the outside world. Hey, no denial here, you had to encapsulate yourself to focus on getting whole!

Examples: Initiate personal contact with someone outside your inner circle, perhaps a favorite co-worker or person that you've been avoiding while you were resurrecting yourself. Participate in conversations with others. Don't allow your conversation to recount what you've been through. You already know that! LISTEN to your friends' ideas and interests and get caught up on what you missed. Catch up on the latest movies.

Step 5 Make a weekly plan to do something with another person. DO NOT automatically find an excuse not to go or talk yourself out of it! DO NOT shortchange your broadening horizons. Continue rebuilding your happy foundation inch by inch.

Check point:
Now, when you glance in the mirror, do you see a sparkle in your eyes and hear yourself say with enthusiasm "I'm back?"
YEAH YOU!!!! If not, go back to step by step techniques to get out of "whatever" land!

Normal sleep patterns are essential and healing. Using sleep to escape life is not. Sleep allows your body to restore itself and recalibrate your tired energy back into vitality. You might want to say, "I'm not productive when I sleep." Yes, you are! Don't be ashamed to sleep when you are using it to heal. Sleep is some of the best "work" you can contribute to healing.

This book encourages an intense, passionate, persistent approach to persevere through your loss "experience." However, it is imperative to choose to be gentle with yourself and require others to do so.

When you have heard all the "be strong" comments you can handle, every so often, announce that you are having a "Gentle Day" which is a mental, emotional, spiritual and physical spa day for the fatigued fighter in you. Even the strongest soldiers need a foot massage, soft words and hugs.

Mark your "Gentle or Me Day" on your calendar. Give yourself the gift of something wonderful soothing and pampering. Celebrate you with a special quiet time or a "happy" event to satisfy and fulfill your spirit.
You've earned it!
You deserve it!!
You're worth it!

Treat yourself and treat yourself right!
Taking care of you, sustains your smile and supports you through the next round.

Balance is as important as recovery.
Cut yourself some slack during your healing regiment. Just don't BE slack about moving forward!

Lessons from Loved Ones in Heaven
How to Connect with your Loved One on the Other Side
to Heal from Loss

Stress and Anxiety

Stress and anxiety is knowing that you have to get up every morning and fight within and with yourself over the effects of this death in your life. You may feel "trapped" by your situation.
Or knowing you have to handle **everything** and keep going and realizing there is no "tooth fairy," it's just up to YOU!

Stress can turn your world upside down before you get out of bed or even begin your journey. It's a survival checklist thing!

You **must** handle anxiety and stress so you can go forward. You must be clear headed and cold hard rational to make the necessary decisions to cover you, your independence and to plan for all the "what ifs" life has to offer in the future.

Getting a grip on stress is essential. **Proaction changes stress into choices** which will preserve your quality of life, independence and survival through this ordeal.

An easy decompressor is physical activity. It's is a simple way to release tension.

However, when dealing with all the overwhelming details just to begin a day, many nervous, agitated, frazzled individuals need help to get "calm." Calm is a very illusive state after loss. Meditation is good for anxiety and de-stressing yourself. Below are methods that take less time with calming results.

Prayer to Be Less Stressed/ Anxious:
I ask and it is my intent for God (or your Higher Power) to remove any doubt and to fill my heart with trust. My mind is anxiety free. I am stress free. So be it, it is done. Thank you.

Affirmation for Stress to Relax and or Sleep.
My mind and heart are filled with Trust. I am relaxed. I am never given more than I can handle. I am blessed with every breath. I am always loved and never alone. Everything is only for my highest and best good. My mind is calm; my body is relaxed. So be it, it is done, Thank you.

Affirmation for Panic Attacks, Heart Palpitations
I command my (fill in the blank Ex: stomach, lung, intestines, bladder, heart) to stabilize now. I command any and all excess, unnecessary, toxic or unhealthy energy to leave my body now and be replaced with physically healing energy. My _____ is stabilized and functioning normally. I am physically healthy. So be it, it is done. Thank you.   Keep repeating this until you are stabilized.

Remember YOUR Choices Create YOUR Consequences! Many people learn to function in their dysfunction and think it's normal. If you tolerate drama, negativity, toxic people and dysfunction in any area of your life then you'll never change what you have decided to tolerate. Choose what you want in your life. It's not about tolerating an existence. Strive for what you want in **all** situations. Make choices that will make it so!

Lessons from Loved Ones in Heaven
How to Connect with your Loved One on the Other Side
to Heal from Loss

Anger is a normal reaction to loss. It depletes emotional stamina and drains your energy. It's self-destructive. You are the only one who chooses to continue to wallow in self-pity and stay stuck in bitterness. Do you want a life like that?

Anger doesn't change anything for the better. When you dwell in the negativity of anger it primarily makes YOU miserable and everyone around you gets the repercussions. It's a struggle that only wears you out!

There are different types of anger. Identify and list any undermining resentments or anger situations that you need to release or just plain get over! Then eliminate them!

Are you mad at God?
"I want my life back!"
"This is so unfair!"
"Why did they take him so soon?"
"Why was this necessary?"
"Why did this have to happen to me?"

Do you take anger (at your situation) out on your family, friends and pets by being snappy, yelling, attacking their ideas and just being ornery?

Remember they're doing the best they can to help understand and support your situation. Plus, they have their own feelings to deal with.

Be kind to Pets, they survive on gut instinct and do nothing but offer unconditional love. They intuitively sense even more keenly than humans exactly what's going on.

After loss, many people live a "fear based life." They feel like the only one taking care of them self and that they have no one to care about or love them back like their beloved did.

After loss, do you feel like everything is a-crisis that must be conquered and resolved right now?

Do you view every opinion to move forward as a criticism which forces you into "a battle to defend yourself"?

Does every opposing thought, action or obstacle in life ignite the warrior in you?

Do you defensively describe yourself as "highly sensitive" to explain away your quicksilver and inconsistent reactive responses?

Do you always bring up the negative side of everything immediately or have an explanation or justification to fend off any and every new idea?

Do you always have a backup and bailout plan?
If yes, then you live a fear based life.

This choice drains you and those around you who always have to be "on guard" against your negativity.

Before you go into "warrior mode" with every situation, adopt an open mind to listen, observe and evaluate. Then you'll have more energy to focus on healing and to prepare for a new balanced future.

However, if you continue to harbor thoughts that "there's no way I'm ever gonna get over this," you are only whirling in your own angry septic tank. That choice can create major depression.

Many people will never have the opportunities, adventures and connection you had with your Loved One. Try transforming that anger into gratitude for all you shared together. I wouldn't trade anything for what Mike and I experienced and **still do**!

View your special Spirit as your copilot or "Team Mikey." That's more factual than "I'm alone and the only one who cares about me" angry defense based attitude. Spirit wants to help you navigate the rest of your life. They got your back forever and ALWAYS! Ask, ask, ask.

Lessons from Loved Ones in Heaven
How to Connect with your Loved One on the Other Side
to Heal from Loss

Depression

Occasionally, a single event can cause a psychological response so intense that it results in a mood low enough that it can be considered a type of depression, anxiety or stress. This condition is referred to as adjustment disorder with depressive features. Usually, and thankfully this condition is temporary.

The MOST important thing is to divert your mind. Keep mentally and or physically busy, busy and busy after you've conquered the initial onslaught of dealing with loss and all that goes with it! Do whatever it takes to reroute your thoughts and redirect your actions. Then discouraging notions will be replaced breath by breath, minute by minute until they are gone!

You MUST replace what you're currently focusing on to defeat depression. Participating in positive stimulating distractions is therapeutic. If you are unable to get going or perform day-to-day activities and that symptom lasts longer than 2 months, please seek help with a grief counselor.

Ever heard the term a "runner's high?" It's a proven fact that exercise puts you in a better mood. Why? Exercise produces chemicals within your body called endorphins that raise your body's chemical levels to make you feel better. Endorphins are released while you are running, working out, walking to keep fit or simply just moving about on a continuous and ongoing basis. Move whatever you've got to lose that mood.

Prayer to Remove Depression
I ask and it is my intent to remove and replace any and all energy and entities in all of time that create (fill in the blank Ex: depression, sadness, irritation,) in my Heart.
I replace that energy with physically healing and loving energy now forevermore and always. So be it, it is done.

Don't forfeit your health and life to personal stagnation or depend on drugs to keep getting you through. Medication may be necessary for a short period of time, but for the rest of your life is inappropriate for living your best self.

It's **your choice** to stop dragging around mentally or physically. It's **your choice** to take control of and broaden your life.

Self-pity is a form of destructive temporary depression. To facilitate getting a better grip on your emotions, break down each day into sections and focus real hard on happy memories and all the good things you shared during that particular timeframe. It allows you to practice being positive. Hopefully you can continuously increase the time spots into days, weeks and then always.

Keep a Daily Thankful Diary Although "happy" might not be how you describe yourself at this point in life, a grateful attitude elevates your outlook to a broader horizon.

Did you know that gratitude raises your energy? Each morning, afternoon and before you go to bed write or think about 1 to 3 things for which you are grateful or have made you happy.

Example: I'm happy I shared my life with my beloved.
I'm glad we took that trip to make memories.
I'm grateful I fostered him during his senior years so he could have lots of love, food, warm belly rubs and treats.

Make a "Happy Book and or Wall"
Do not call it a memory or remembrance book. What you **did** (i.e. the activity) together created an earth memory, but your special Spirit is alive and well and definitely not a memory. In fact you can

even create a journal of your new journey with Spirit if you choose.

This task will produce a mindset that **looks** for gifts and enthusiastic events, rather than doom gloom. Post pictures and narrate the journey you shared.

When you have a not-so-good day, reread the positives you wrote. Do not neglect your "Happy" project. However, don't make this a chore. When your outlook is sinking flip through the pages or go look at the wall or area. It will refocus your mind on the good times shared and you can have a positive cleansing cry if necessary.

If you cover a wall with all the photos that make you smile, walk by it often to uplift your heart. You can also create an area or designate a sacred space with their earth suit ashes and mementos. Just don't forget that y'all are now beginning a new life journey together in a different form.

Memorial Area

Many people create a shrine area, memorial garden, or sacred space for their pet or person. They think this space is the best place to connect. NOT so, because Spirit is with you **wherever** you are.

Be careful that you do not get so attached to this memorial area and all of the stuff in it that it affects your moving forward. It's just a place with earth "remains."

I became obsessed with my engagement ring and all of Mike's photos. Touch any of those and I was in your face. I believed that if I lost a photo, did not wear his ring or didn't wear, sleep with or keep various pieces of clothing that I would be forever disconnected and disassociated from him. I've learned beyond that obsessive and compulsive behavior. Mike was just waiting for **me** to catch up with a new view!

A warning about shrines and memorial areas is especially true for pet bereavement. Pet parents often believe there is an actual place called Rainbow Bridge. It's a 1980's poem that created a fantasy **make believe** heavenly residence! It's NOT real! Rainbow Bridge named web sites and businesses encourage posting "dead pet" stuff and ceremonies. Many individuals think they're honoring their pet by paying for products like paying for a "residence" in a pretend place, or photos sprouting wings with halos, saying I'm waiting for you or memorial flowers on an imaginary RB gravesite. Heaven is FREE!

A Rainbow Bridge reality check upsets some pet parents' belief systems. They are unable to step out of fictional facts for fear of losing connection with their pet. Their choice of this imaginary belief is what shuts everything down with a real living Spirit connection and ongoing life.

Why is this important to address? Watching people suffer unnecessary grief under false premises is heart wrenching. When you become aware of life after death you realize that your Person or Pet is not dead and gone. And "waiting for you" to die to "join them" is also false. Spirit validates never ending love and a continuous relationship through your ongoing communication and connection.

Memorials

The purpose for "memorials," a funeral, religious service or wake is to honor and celebrate the life of your beloved. If you choose uplifting verbiage like "Celebrating the life of," that phrasing is more inspirational and correct. Memorial services are inherently designed to help everyone feel better and to accept that your beloved has moved on.

Lessons from Loved Ones in Heaven
How to Connect with your Loved One on the Other Side
to Heal from Loss

During the service your Loved One is usually there being appreciative of all those who came to honor their life. I never knew this until I was asked to walk to the front of the church for Mike's service to begin. I didn't have the courage.

So, there I am huddling in the back of the church wearing my proper black suit clutching Mike's framed photo and crying behind his sunglasses. I cried "Mike I can't do this, you have to go with me!"

Suddenly, a wave of warm love and a peaceful safe feeling poured all around me like fudge over ice cream. I knew it was Mike wrapping me in his arms to give me the strength to go on, and so we did! He stayed by my side throughout the entire ceremony, burial and drive home.

If the memorial triggers an emotional upheaval, don't inflict your sadness on others. Take time to take care of you, it's normal, natural and necessary. Don't consciously pull someone else "down" just because you are. Talk about it. Suppressing emotions at this time is not good.

Go deep into your heart feelings to find their love space. Remember how your love and happiness felt. You can savor all those special memories by yourself whenever and wherever you are, and no one can take that from you- ever!

I keep Mike's love in a special heart space. When life is overbearing, I summon those special feelings to surround me so I can keep on keeping on. I ask him to be with me, to protect me, and to help me get through whatever it is I have to face.

Since you can recognize your special Spirit's energy presence, remember, you are never alone. Spirit wants to be there for you. ASK!

Tattoos

After Transition, you will be grasping for anything to hold onto the special bond you shared.

"Ink" or "tats "can be a permanent remembrance. You might want to rethink a few things before you make the design.

Only the earth suit is a memory. Tattooing "in memory of" is incorrect because Spirits are **not a memory** but living energy.

Try using "Celebrating our Love" because that is factual and positive. Or "our love is everlasting" or "continuing our love," or "forever and always" or "never ending love." All these slogans are real facts and will be more uplifting than the incorrect traditional verbiage.

Only the earth suit is subject to dates of existence, so you might want to leave that part off too.

Lessons from Loved Ones in Heaven
How to Connect with your Loved One on the Other Side
to Heal from Loss

Creating an Uplifting Environment

Reshaping depression caused by a Death is all encompassing. Everywhere you look, it reminds you of your beloved companion. Don't underestimate how much your environment can contribute to your recovery. It's your haven, a sanctuary, your hide-a-way and your greatest subliminal support system.

The general rule is to try to maintain your normal lifestyle. Don't make any **major** life changes (for example, moving, changing jobs, changing important relationships) during the first year of bereavement. This will let you keep your roots and some sense of security.

You can however shapeshift a few things to help you heal and initiate new life patterns.

Personal Space
Open those curtains! It's scientifically proven that sunlight helps alleviate depression. Looking out windows encourages you to feel less "trapped" and invites you to think about what you are viewing.

Despite your current circumstances, don't let discouragement deter you from enjoying some person, thing or event every day. Encourage folks to visit and participate in activities that nourish, uplift and satisfy your inner joy.

Think about a waiting room with lots of sick folks, then think about your favorite restaurant on the ocean or in the mountains with someone fun. Which thought aroused inner happiness? Replay the happies!

Freshen up the décor! Use cheerful paint, fabrics and colorful pillows to enliven your living area. Loving your surroundings helps take your mind off the "experience." "Favorite and fun stuff" can play an essential part in enriching your living right now!

You can be sad while sleeping on red satin or leopard print sheets in a pretty peignoir set with feathered mule scuffies. On the other hand, you can rest in stained, smelly worn out sheets, rarely washed t-shirts and sweat pants and clean up only "when you go out." Either way you are still "experiencing" your loss issue. Your self-esteem and mood will be boosted the more enthusiastic you are about your appearance and activities!

"Experiencing" loss is a great excuse to break out of your normal "style" to try something wonderful and new! You might want to read a Feng Shui (the Chinese art of placement and space arrangement of furniture to promote a harmonious environment) book to learn how to position your furniture so it can also facilitate healing. Go for it! Blame it on being crazy dealing with all you are going through.

Comfort Foods
Right after a funeral people bring food, really good food. That's nice for a while! Don't get so into comfort food and libations that you grow in size. It would be greatly disappointing for your Loved One to see you wreck your life by mouth. Spirit always wants you to be healthy and happy, even when you're unaware -**Spirit is watching**.

In readings, I've had many clients be told by Spirit to stop smoking. One Lop Eared bunny told her mother that she was sneaking out behind the garage to smoke so it wouldn't hurt the bunny. The bunny told her get rid of that habit because it was nasty and harming her.

Another Spirit told the husband to stop having all those extra cocktails, stop being so lazy and quit being sloppy i.e. dropping food all over the house, leaving dishes sitting around and living in his underwear and flip flops. Ironically many clients have responded, "well I wouldn't do this for myself, but I'll do it for my person or pet in Spirit.

Sound Therapy
Every sound has a specific frequency. Certain sound combinations (music, soothing tones, even drumming) can help alter your mood! There are sound tones and music CD's that have been scientifically formulated for healing. It's a great way to support mental health!

Aromatherapy Makes Scents!
Unless medically prohibited, check out aromatherapy, scented oils, candles (lemon candles are said to draw only good vibes). If medically safe, use your favorite perfume (even on your pillow), scented aerosols in the room, pot pourri or have fresh flowers. It's a proven fact that smells can trigger the brain to produce various actions within your body and activate positive memories. Choose scents that please you and create a delightful memory and environment. Mike's Spirit used to manifest his special cologne as a Sign to make me smile.

Color Therapy
Surround yourself with soothing colors and pleasant paintings. Did you know that **every color has a measurable energy that affects** your moods, your mental processes and your body's reaction?

Art medicine and healing art in healthcare facilities is a rapidly growing industry. I am a pioneer in evidence based art medicine and art for health by scientifically and alternatively documenting the healing benefits and diagnostic abilities of my Paintings that Heal®. Check out my website www.BrentAtwater.com.

Clothing Therapy
Don't look or dress like you are "a victim of loss!"

Get rid of that ratty old bathrobe that looks and smells- OUT, OUT, OUT! Being disheveled stymies your progress, depresses your mood and creates a negative reminder for everyone around you. Retrain your mind and reframe your personal image to exemplify you have a life to lead.

After Mike died I bought clothes way too large for me that were "comfortable" in dark colors. I hid behind my clothing. I thought that if I was invisible or unpleasant then no one would want to interact with me and that was perfect. People could just leave me alone and I could suffer in silence. I didn't have to be chirpy at the grocery store, pleasant in the mall or on the street while walking the dog. Just cover me up and I'd disappear.

I lived disguised that way until someone set me up with a widower for a blind afternoon meeting at year 10.

I'm a size 4 so I got my best medium to large not too revealing outfit out and dressed up. And why bother with make up? He could take me as I was or go home. The later idea actually sounded pretty good. Forget touching up my roots, it was only dinner.

Ring door bell. Open door. I say "hello," and he says, "They told me you were an attractive ex-NY model who is really a fun person. I wasn't expecting a frumpy 90-year-old having a bad hair day." (exact words)

Mind you, I sorta thought I was doing the best I could, while still honoring Mike's memory.

His words were a wake-up call!
So, I scanned his person and retorted "and with your bad dyed hair (you know that orange red brown at the white temples look) and 70's disco lounge lizard polyester shirt and too tight pants with Done Laps disorder (i.e. belly over the belt), you are not exactly a striking gentleman."

This began our ongoing friendship. He ruffled up at me and said, "I'm leaving." I said, "I'm glad" and that was that until he re-rang the doorbell an hour later.

I asked why he was back and he said it was his fault we got off to a bad start. I agreed and confessed to my participation in our demise.

I then invited him in and we sat in the kitchen for over 5 hours and talked about how life had changed after the death of our spouses, and how we didn't know how to do this "date thing.".

It was a "pour your soul out" event that was cathartic and life changing for both of us with our raw, key word, raw, open vulnerable tell it like it is sincerity. We decided to start again. Have another first date and dress appropriately like we would have **before** the death of our significant other.

He drove up in his silver-grey Mercedes convertible, with gorgeous thick salt and pepper hair that all men want at "that age." It enhanced his ice blue eyes even more. And was he dressed! Amen! Dressed elegant country club casual so befitting a Southern Gentleman. Obviously, some personal shopper from a gentleman haberdasher's shop had helped him and it was all good!

I bought make up and practiced using it with the newest looks until I felt better about myself (key) felt better about myself. Then I read all the fashion mags and determined what I would and could wear best that was age appropriate. And I cut and colored my hair to be "with it."

His initial response when I opened the door "WOW, that's what I expected to see the first time we met." I blushed for the first time in years and actually had a fleeting moment of nervousness because my Soul knew it was moving forward and I was beginning to like myself again. I almost felt guilty about feeling that way. DON'T feel guilty you're moving forward in the healing process.

I complimented his achievements and swag and later we began many long discussions on how to get through this phase of our lives. We taught each other to re-find the best of ourselves.

How you see YOURSELF affects your mood!
Dress healthy, even if you have to fake yourself out for a while in order to lift yourself up!

When you start feeling better and more secure in going forward, wear invigorating happy bright colors, not gravestone grey and funeral black. There are "happy color" outfits that are waiting for you which will fit into any budget. Try wearing green (for healing), pink (for love), blue (for peace), yellow (for cheerfulness), power red (life force energy) or vacation ocean turquoise, regal purple and other colors you always liked. If you want to try that hot pink, chartreuse, sheer, fluffy, ruffled, sexy, lacy or flowered extravagant whatever, do it! New you, new life.

If medically safe, change your hair color, paint those nails, get a pedicure and wear that bright coral lipstick. NOW is the time. The compliments you receive about your appearance will be wonderfully uplifting and a validation that you are getting you back!

Plus, when you walk by the mirror, you can say to yourself "at least I look better than I feel." Grab your chance to step out of your fashion comfort zone into your "gosh I'd like to try wearing that."

By kicking your wardrobe color into high gear; it'll help you be more vivacious when you're down!

Go for it if it makes you smile, and that brings us to the following subject:

Laughter Therapy

You've got a lot to handle and I know you don't feel like smiling much less laughing.

However, in time, you and your close friends go to a favorite restaurant and recount happy times or stay home and binge on fun DVD's that lift your mood. It will be a good thing for your well-being and another positive step towards recovery.

A 1997 Loma Linda study validates that laughter raises the chemical levels in your body's immune system response by increasing the number of natural germ killer cells. Laughter also lowers your blood pressure and raises your endorphins plus expands your arteries. Stress constricts them. A happy and positive person lives longer and handles life better.

In the book Eat, Pray, Love, "happiness is the result of personal effort," and not a "stroke of luck." "You fight for it, strive for it, insist upon it." I totally agree. Try it!

Happiness is a choice. This can be one of your reentry goals.

Guilt

No matter what happened surrounding the death of your Person or Pet, everything was exactly as **both of you** planned for that particular time and exit point!!!
I know, what a thing to say!

That's the spiritual perspective. It's now time to start examining events from your new view. Here's the basic premise. Your time on Earth is the Universal school where your Soul learns lessons and evolves to a higher and more aware understanding about all of life.

Under that premise, you made the right decisions, you did not give up on your beloved, or not be there when you were supposed to be, or overlook something, or not step up at the right time. Everything was chosen by both of you and pre-scripted.

Choose to forgive and release yourself for all the things you did or didn't say or do. Compassion for yourself and others is important in healing.

There was nothing that should, could or would have been changed for the learning opportunities each of your souls chose to experience. Please **reread** that until you have that concept imprinted in your DNA.

Guilt is a self-focused emotion. You're beating yourself up. It dilutes the focus on loss because you are so preoccupied with YOUR guilt that it helps justify your pain.

Explaining away your pain through guilt is only a cover up of how deeply you loved, care and feel. It's healthy to own the latter emotions and give up the inappropriate self-focused guilt.

Everything is a Soul lesson you both agreed to experience in this lifetime.

If you still feel guilt, then examine even more closely what you learned from that transition experience. Your knowledge is the EXACT education you were supposed to be taught by each other. Take your new-found comprehension and realize your Soul and life has evolved to a higher level. Talk to your Spirit about this for ever further clarity.

Understanding "why" a death occurred **is the Gift** contained within that traumatic event!! These worst moments give you a chance for your biggest growth.

Yeah right you say. I said the same thing for 10 years until I understood that the "Gift" was for my

Soul's highest and best evolution, NOT my earth suit life gratification.

Nothing bad can ever seem good. How you deal with the bad event or thing is the choice and consequence factor. Stop looking at this death as a negative guilt laden ending. Spiritually embrace this death – transition scenario as the lesson that expands your awareness about your ongoing journey together.

Another form of feeling guilty is because you're sensing that you're beginning to move forward a little. You might think you're deserting and dishonoring your beloved's memory. Not so. Spirit wants you to be happy and loved and enjoy your time on Earth.

Some individuals take oppressive depression and guilt about the loss to a level that makes them want to think about leaving Earth. That's normal for a split second but not any longer.

Suicide is NOT a choice or remedy endorsed or condoned by Spirit.

Dealing with Loss by Suicide

If you're heartbroken because your beloved died by choosing to end their life, here's what you need to know. Do not have guilt.

It was their Soul's choice to leave earth.
It's **their Soul's path**.

YOU are **only** responsible for **your** Soul's choices.

Suicidal Thoughts

In today's world, you can feel invisible in a relationship, workplace, educational facility, religious venue, recreational meeting area or home environment. It's easy to feel lost and perhaps even wonder "who gives a <u>bleep</u> about me?"

You may hold the impression that the only ones who care about your existence are maybe your friends, family and pets. When a Person or Pet in that support community dies, you may feel like you have no kindred soul to share with, a heart connection to validate your existence, much less others who are really concerned about your wellbeing and want to give you a hug and listen to what you have to say.

The Person or Pet that transitioned is your "everything" and "reason to live." At that point, it may cross your mind to consider leaving too! These thoughts are real!

Please tell someone or confide in your best supportive person **immediately if** you are entertaining and sorting through details to join your beloved Pet or Person.

There is nothing to be ashamed about.
You just need assistance in coping with major grief. It's normal!

If you look at death and it seems friendly and a "relief" you **need URGENT help.** You <u>MUST</u> get professional help so they can assist you in sorting this out.

If you are finalizing the plans to facilitate your demise, **GET HELP   NOW.**

Call the National Suicide Prevention Lifeline
1-800-273-8255   Always open!
There are free grief counselors and groups so money is not an excuse or issue.

Don't be afraid to tell someone how you are feeling and thinking.
Don't be afraid to share your plans and ideas about death with another person. Then someone will have your back and you'll not feel as alone.

EVERYONE has dealt with a death in their lifetime. **There IS someone who has felt like you do now.** They **can totally understand** and **help you through** this horrific time!

It's especially hard to handle a death when you are disabled or surviving alone with no support and your Person or Pet is the **only** being you have on Earth that matters. Oftentimes family, friends, partners, relatives, lovers, coworkers or others just "don't get it!"

Therefore, it may appear that there is nothing or no one else to turn to. WRONG!!

I understand where you are coming from and how you feel. Thoughts about leaving are sad and hopeful all at the same time. You figure it's a way out of your pain. **It's not!**

I admit that I thought about leaving to join Mike. The only thing that kept me here was my pets. And when my pets died, what was the point in me staying after that?
Well there is a point!

Take a deep breath and give me a chance to offer you some **reasons to stay.**

You need to stay on earth to tell folks about your Pet or Person and the wonderful life and stories you shared. Otherwise they will go unremembered.

Spiritually speaking, you'll have to come back in another lifetime and learn how to conquer your demons for your Soul's evolution.
I chose to stay and work it out!!!
Now I don't have to do it all over nor re-experience the death pain and scenario again in another lifetime.

Look at the People and Pets you would leave behind that need your strength and living example to get them through this loss.
Stay for them!

Pet Parents, if you leave and your pet returns/reincarnates, who will he come back too?   See YouTube video 138.

If you feel like "This is just devastating my life."
You need perspective! It devastates your life **ONLY if you choose to allow it** to do so.
Ask your beloved Spirit how to eradicate victim mentality!

How to shapeshift negative thoughts and comments
Do you say, "I don't have any hope left?"
Add "at this time."
Hope IS the human spirit. You have the inner strength to get through this. Even if you don't believe you can and you lack passion for having a life- **at this time**-, there still is hope. That's why each day provides a new start.

I just can't do this anymore." Add, **"at this time"** or, **"In a few minutes I will be better."**
Leave a window of opportunity open for improvement.
If you shut any opportunity out of your mind, YOU stop the possibility!

Emptiness

When all is said and done and settling down, emptiness usually sets in. That quiet no noise, raw vacant place in your mind, heart, soul and house begins to start messing with your mind! Everything, everybody, every activity and even you are just void or filled with nothingness.

You will always have a scar in your heart for the Person or Pet's earth suit. They were and **are** a part of your Soul's journey.

Emptiness for the earth suit is like a blinking light. It will flicker on and off for the rest of your lifetime. Why? To remind you of all the wonderful things you shared together which are etched in your Soul and interwoven among the fibers of your being. Your heart will blink when you are touched by a memory or their Spirit is near. See YouTube video 10

Hugs and kisses, smells and touching are a wonderful earth sensory bonus. However, in time, interaction with their physical form will be less and less important as you enjoy hugs and kisses, smells and touching their Spirit form.

In the distant future, you'll never feel alone when you're living in a retirement or continuing care facility because you'll know how to connect with and talk to your beloved Spirit who'll be right there with you!! Think about all the people in a nursing home who feel so alone. You won't be one.

Another method to help fill the emptiness is to surround yourself with people who view you through the eyes of their heart!

My mother came to breakfast one morning very disheveled. She said she didn't sleep well the night before and asked how she looked. I responded truthfully, that she was not very attractive and suggested make up would do the trick. To my amazement, my father responded, "I think you look beautiful."

Being the very candid person that I am, I asked him why in the world would he say that. With a smile, he declared: "I look at your mother with my heart and I think she is beautiful."

I learned a very important lesson. Surround yourself with people who are in tune with you through their heart. These special individuals will sense, support, uplift and understand your emptiness and respond appropriately.

New Relationships

Now that you have a relationship with Spirit, what does the future look like with other relationships?

"Without them" is not factual except for the "suit." Spirit is with and near you anytime you choose. "Irreplaceable" is a valid comment because no energy is the same. You have the choice to enjoy new companionship or not.

Everyone asks, "How will you be with the next man in your life?" I explain that he will benefit from all the lessons I learned in my relationship with Mike. Your new Pet or Person will benefit from your learning and get an even better version of you to love.

Ask Spirit to direct you to the perfect new Person or Pet. Spirit knows what makes you happy.

Mike wanted me to start dating so I wouldn't be alone. I said "I only love you." He said "I want you to be happy. Our love will always be special just between us. Any new love will be a different experience and will never compete with what we have." I accepted my first date.

During New Year's Eve, over dessert, David asked if I wanted to go out again and start dating.
I felt uncomfortable in even thinking that I might want to do so. At that moment, Mike's Spirit stood up directly behind David's chair and said, "tell him yes."

Mike then informed me that "you'll be dating him for 2 years. You need to have some fun and he needs your help." I about lost it! Trying to remain calm, I nonchalantly replied "that would be nice." Mike's Spirit then vanished.

What you need to know
Spirit wants you to continue to experience all the good that you shared with them.
Share love and being loved
Have companionship and fun
Be healthy and happy.

No new Pet or Person is going to upset your Loved One. Spirit will not get mad, feel disrespected, replaced or unloved. No new relationship will run them off or change what you have together.

You can however, dishonor your beloved by choosing to shut your mind to their participation in your healing and ongoing life. Spirit wants to love, help, protect and guide you for your best life. Spirit has your best interests at heart.

Refining your Rebuilding

Look how much **you have grown**. Adding a few more perspectives will also help reshape a better future.

Being Grateful
Being grateful is a perspective that will prevent you from "getting down on yourself."
Be glad you had the time together. Celebrate sharing!

Helping Others
When earth memories/ experiences sneak back in and become too raw, you can always honor your Spirit by passing the Love your shared forward.

Since Mike's transition ignited my Gifts further, I decided to share the caring he made me feel inside by extending that caring for others. I get up every day and assist people who are dealing with death so no one will feel alone like I did. It's my mission.

Now my days are spent passing forward the good I experienced from Mike into inspiring and lifting another who is going through what I experienced. That adds purpose to my life.

Choosing to help others is one of the last steps in moving forward into "loss adjustment." That's quite a word after all you've gone through.

Reaching out and helping someone else in the condition you endured and survived is where you choose to share vulnerable truths, fears and victories which strengthens you and the other person. It also allows you to view your turmoil from another perspective that is educational and teaches you even more about yourself.

Use your "experience" to contribute to and benefit others. Allow your beloved's "love light" lessons to shine through your future actions and activities to honor them.
If you inspire or help only **one** Person or Pet, **your life has made a difference!**

Are you ever healed?
Yes, your Soul evolves to a greater understanding, clarity and awareness by your choices.

Do you ever recover?
Recovery is returning to a normal state of health, mind, or strength. You'll always have the lessons you learned about transition etched in your heart and part of your Soul's evolutionary journey.

You'll "recover" however those loss lessons will contribute to the substance of who you are as a new person.

It boils down to this
The Choices you make through grief and bereavement create the consequences of your Soul's gowth and future path!

Your state of mind determines the quality of your life.

"Young souls learn to accept responsibility for their actions.
Mature souls learn to accept responsibility for their thoughts. And old souls learn to accept responsibility for their happiness."

Notes from The Universe

Lessons from Loved Ones in Heaven
How to Connect with your Loved One on the Other Side
to Heal from Loss

I hope my book has given you the inspiration, techniques and tools to transform your life and your initial position on this chart!

STAGES OF GRIEF

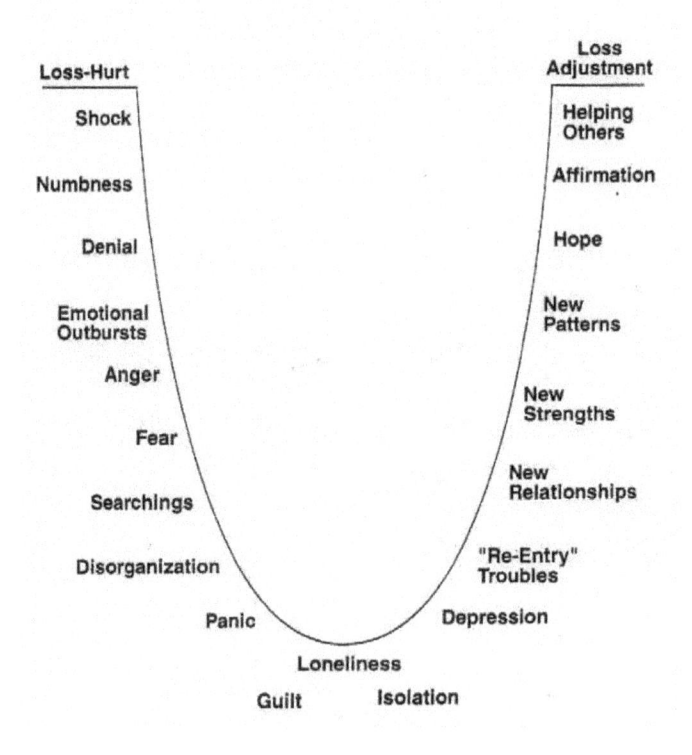

Loss-Hurt
Shock
Numbness
Denial
Emotional Outbursts
Anger
Fear
Searchings
Disorganization
Panic
Guilt
Loneliness
Isolation
Depression
"Re-Entry" Troubles
New Relationships
New Strengths
New Patterns
Hope
Affirmation
Helping Others
Loss Adjustment

In conclusion

I asked Spirits what to say. Here's what I got.

Give yourself time to grieve, it's human,
but tend to your Heart light.
Go forward honoring your beloved and enjoying the
new journey with "all there is" in love and
happiness. That's what They want for you!

In your darkest hours ask your special Spirit to
communicate and connect with you to heal your
heart, expand your awareness and rebuild your future
together! Ask for their advice and help, they know
you best of all!

Fill your life with awesome experiences!!
No earth suit lasts forever,
Spirits are eternal!

Know, after Transition, connection and
communication is perpetual and **real.**

Love is Never Ending!
As Mike says, **"Forever & Always!"**

Message to Book Clubs, Professional Associations and Organizations

I'd be honored to speak with your group over the phone or in person.
We can also discuss a Live Event in your area.
Email: Brent@brentatwater.com

Messages to Individuals

Yes, I have Readings that communicate with your Loved Ones. Visit my website
www. BrentAtwater.com

RESOURCES

1. Facebook Groups:
People Loss Group
Missing Loved Ones in Heaven & Afterlife In loving memory <3

Pet Loss Group World's # 1 Animal life after death Group.

Animal Life after Death, Pet Loss, Afterlife Sign, Reincarnation <3 Answers

Professional Bereavement Counselor
Frankie Johnson's contact info is on my website.

2. YouTube Channel -Brent Atwater

3. Pet Loss Radio & Podcasts Show "Alive Again" on www.PetLifeRadio.com

4. After Death Communication Blog
http://petreincarnation.blogspot.com. Share your stories

5. Workshops, Events / Live Q & A Chats are announced on Brent Atwater's LIVE Facebook Page, Group and Website.

6. Live Events: Want an Event in your area-email us!

Memorial Wristband:

Engraved: My Love is Never Ending. I'm coming back to YOU! ™
These can be found on my website.

Translations: We have Translators for our Facebook pages, Groups, YouTube videos and personal Readings.

Lessons from Loved Ones in Heaven
How to Connect with your Loved One on the Other Side
to Heal from Loss

Lessons from Loved Ones in Heaven
How to Connect with your Loved One on the Other Side
to Heal from Loss

Brent Atwater

Brent Atwater and "Friend" her dog with a "B" on his Bottom, are the world's authority on animal life after death, Afterlife signs and reincarnation. Brent's readings are filled with very personal information and specific details that provide answers, comfort, peace, clarity and closure that captivate clients and audiences around the world.

As a medical intuitive, Ms. Atwater also has the extraordinary Gift to see inside a body to accurately diagnose current and future health issues and to create healing solutions.

At age 5 Brent's intuitive talents were discovered by Duke University's Dr. J. B. Rhine the founder of ESP in his initial investigations. Ms. Atwater's specialized intuitive diagnostic abilities have earned her the nickname of the "human MRI."

Her world renowned Medical Intuitive practice has highly respected, evidence based, documented and published case studies. Brent can see the organs, nerves, bones, tissue et al inside your body, plus diagnose and predict future events. Therefore Ms. Atwater can also determine when your pet is going to reincarnate and what they will look like!

Brent's healing work regenerating her dog's spinal cord nerves and vertebra has been documented by NC State University's School of Veterinary Medicine. She has been a speaker and teacher for the NC Veterinary Association and taught at the New York Open Center. For decades Ms. Atwater has pioneered and founded AIH the field of Animal Intuitive Healthcare & Healing. Her Medical Intuitive Diagnosis MIDI and AIH books are groundbreaking resource books for the science of

Medical Intuition and Healing Animals with Integrative Energy Medicine.

In 1987 Brent founded the Just Plain Love® Charitable Trust. After law school and the death of her fiancé, Brent refocused her career on helping pets and their people heal. Ms. Atwater has authored 11 Just Plain Love® Books with more to follow.

Ms. Atwater has devoted decades to researching life after death, reincarnation and human animal spiritual contracts which produced multiple books whose titles are translated into other languages.

Brent offers us the benefit of her incredible Gifts and her passion to help heal and uplift the lives of pets and their people! Her mission is to ignite hope and healing in people and to activate and empower every person's inherent abilities and Gifts.

Ms. Atwater is also a pioneer in healing art medicine by scientifically documenting the healing energy, diagnostic abilities and healing benefits of her Paintings That Heal® (www.BrentAtwater.com). She is one of the contemporary American painters who are bringing forth a new cultural renaissance by blending her classical artistic training with spirituality and energy infused into her healing art.

Lessons from Loved Ones in Heaven
How to Connect with your Loved One on the Other Side
to Heal from Loss

Brent Atwater's life work facilitates positive and transformative results!

"Friend" is the co-host of Brent's life!

He is a Red tri colored Border collie. Friend "B"elieves his mission is to expand awareness about animal life after death to help heal hearts. When he's not assisting Brent with paw signings, pet fund raising events or practicing hugs and kisses for his pet therapy work, Friend enjoys being spoiled, walking by the river to find Mr. Bunny, herding fish and turtles in his pond and playing with his "Mister Bears."

Lessons from Loved Ones in Heaven
How to Connect with your Loved One on the Other Side
to Heal from Loss

Lessons from Loved Ones in Heaven
How to Connect with your Loved One on the Other Side
to Heal from Loss

Join Brent Atwater's Global Community on, Facebook, YouTube, Twitter, Instagram, Snapchat, LinkedIn, Pinterest, Periscope and others.

Lessons from Loved Ones in Heaven
How to Connect with your Loved One on the Other Side
to Heal from Loss

Just Plain Love® Books
inspiring thoughts that provide smiles, hugs and healing for every reader's heart!

Other Just Plain Love® Titles
Inspirational:
The Beach Book: Beach Lessons for a Workaholic!

Children's Books:
Cancer Kids—God's Special Children!
Cancer and MY Daddy

Life and Spiritual Purpose:
How to Accept, Trust & Live Your Life's Spiritual Purpose: Am I Worthy?
Prayers to Empower Your Life's Spiritual Purpose

Energy Medicine, Intuitive Development:
Medical Intuition, Intuitive Diagnosis, MIDI- How to See Inside a Body to Diagnose, Treat & Heal
AIH - Animal Intuitive Healthcare & Healing for Veterinarians, Assistants & Technicians

Self Help and Healing, Mind Body Medicine:
Healing Yourself! 23 Ways to Heal YOU!

Lessons from Loved Ones in Heaven, How to Connect with your Loved One on the Other Side to Heal from Loss

Pet Loss, Afterlife, Animal Life after Death
After Death Signs from Pet Afterlife and Animals in Heaven

Lessons from Loved Ones in Heaven
How to Connect with your Loved One on the Other Side
to Heal from Loss

Animal Reincarnation
Animal Life after Death
the Dog with a "B" on His Bottom!
"I'm Home!" a Dog's Never-Ending Love Story
"I'm Home!" a Cat's Never-Ending Love Story
"Pet Loss, Afterlife & Pet Life after Death!
La Réincarnation des Animaux de Compagnie
動物は生まれ変わる

This material is internationally copyrighted with all rights reserved to B. Brent Atwater. None of this material may be used or reproduced without written permission of B. Brent Atwater. © 2008-2018 R1